Oft in the Chilly Night

Oft in the Chilly Night

Molly Tomeltey

ATHENA PRESS
LONDON

*In memory of our parents and our brother,
this memoir is dedicated
to my four sisters.
(I know you will not mind my raking over
the ashes of our youth).
To the 'Hanleys' and the 'Hanrahans',
and to any other old friends who may see something
of themselves in these pages.*

Contents

Oft in the stilly night
Ere slumber's chain hath bound me,
Fond memory brings the light
Of other days around me.

Thomas Moore 1779–1852

What You Are About to Receive

> Oft in the chilly night
> Ere slumber's chain hath bound me,
> Its clanking giveth me a fright—
> Put another blanket round me.

My apologies to Tom Moore![1] At least his second line came out all right. So what do I, a Jumpy Old Woman, do when I cannot sleep at night? I think about the past. First, I go back to 1935, the year in which my memory began to kick in. Then I go over my clearest memories of the next ten years, from my third to my thirteenth year. I relive my childhood, my full-strength Irish Catholic childhood, and believe it or not, it was happy.

I don't, then, look back in anger[2], but in joy and thankfulness – and maybe with an occasional dash of mischief. For I think we have lately had too many harrowing tales from this background. Indeed, we have supped too full of horrors in these ancestral halls![3] It must be time for some plain fare of the bread and butter kind. (But who – you may well ask – is going to swallow that?)

I have no axe to grind, no skeleton to let out, no dark secret to reveal, no can of worms to open. You won't find anything very unsavoury here. I may spill a bean or two, let the odd kitten out of the odd bag, but that's about the size of it. What's on the menu is simply a slice of ordinary life. However, it does have all the ingredients on Wordsworth's list:

> For human nature's daily food,
> For transient sorrows, simple wiles
> Praise, blame, love, kisses, tears and smiles.[4]

Notes

[1] Thomas Moore (1779–1852): Irish poet. His best-known work, *Irish Melodies,* (1807–34) includes 'Oft in the Stilly Night' and 'The Last Rose of Summer'. Moore was as famous in his time as Sir Walter Scott and Lord Byron, who left him his manuscript *Memoirs*, to be published after his death.

[2] *Look Back in Anger*: the play by John Osborne (1929–94) that came out in 1956 and broke new ground in English drama. The phrase has now passed into common use.

[3] 'supped too full of horrors': allusion to *Macbeth*, Act V, Scene v. 'I have supp'd full with horrors.' (allusion also to some recent accounts of tragic Irish childhoods).

[4] 'For human nature's daily food': quotation from the poem 'She was a phantom of delight' by William Wordsworth (1770–1850).

My Family

My parents, Timmy and Tessa Tomeltey, were married in 1929, and by 1942 had five daughters and one son.

My sister Catherine was born first, in 1930. She was an early talker and had an outgoing personality. She was something of an *enfant terrible* who once, famously, lifted her dress to show the Canon her new knickers. Because these knickers had a pocket she felt they deserved a wider audience. She showed them also to a bar customer who gave her a coin to put in the pocket. This gave her a business idea but our mother caught her when she tried it out again. That put paid to that idea.

I looked up to her, regarding her as a kind of 'super sister'. I suppose that was because, like my parents, she had always been there. My father liked to tell us of the time he found her, poised over my cot, about to shave me with his cut-throat razor. That was a close shave for me! Come to think of it, I could do with her services in that area nowadays. She kept me well under her thumb and made me do all kinds of things. Once she made me take a sip out of the chamber pot. It wasn't nice, I assure you. How strange that some eminent, oriental gentlemen should have considered this liquid therapeutic.

I, Molly, came next after Catherine, in 1932. This was also the year that made Éamon de Valera Taoiseach[5] of the Irish Free State[6], brought the Eucharistic Congress to the city of Dublin, added *Brave New World* and *Cold Comfort Farm* to the body of English Literature, and put Caesar Salad on the tables of Mexico. (I mention only a few of the significant events of that momentous year.) I was the quiet one; the silent listener under the counter – until my cover was blown.

With the birth of my sister Bernadette in 1935, my memory was jerked into full working order. I believe that my first completely clear memory is of that event. I was not, of course, present at it, but when I reached the landing I knew that something was going on behind the red door of my mother's room. I looked through the keyhole and saw a woman washing a baby in the tin tub my mother did the clothes washing in. There was no washboard though. When I couldn't open the door I kicked it and screamed. Then my father arrived on the landing and carried me off, still kicking and screaming. That woman, whom I saw through the keyhole, became a familiar figure to me over the next few years. Her name was Nurse Noonan, purveyor of babies to town and country.

Bernadette clung to her bedtime bottle for longer than usual. She wasn't going to be fobbed off with a 'rotten orange',[7] whatever age she'd reached. After her first day at school she reported to my mother that Miss McGinty had blessed herself with her left hand. She was scandalised. It was almost an article of faith at home that you made the Sign of the Cross with your right hand. Yet here was the teacher doing the wrong thing. Of course, when facing a class of infants, a teacher got a better response by using her left hand. Nevertheless our Bernadette immediately spotted the deliberate ploy, which I wouldn't have seen at her age in a month of Sundays.

On another occasion, on returning to school after lunch, the principal asked her what she'd had to eat. Bernadette told her we'd had a crow. That got a rare laugh from Miss Hanrahan. Dire as those times certainly were, we hadn't quite come to that.

July 1937 was a trying month for my parents. I had scarlet fever, and because of this my brother Joseph had to be born in hospital – the only one of us not born at home. (I understood, years later, that an unholy row had occurred between the hospital authorities on one side, and my parents and their doctor on the other. It appears that my mother, having been in contact with scarlet fever, was a danger to other patients. Expensive arrangements had to be made, and the hospital authorities were furious.) My father had had typhoid, or something similar, in 1919, so it was considered safe for him, and only him, to nurse me. I remember how sore my throat was. On one visit the doctor pressed my tongue down, to get a good look, using a spoon. It could hardly have been the size of a tablespoon, but that's what it felt like. To this day a tablespoon can make me retch.

As I got better, my skin began to come off. At first I was alarmed at the sight, until I saw I had another layer of skin underneath. Then, when I found it didn't hurt, I enjoyed peeling it off. It came in shreds and strips. I tried to make as long a strip as I could. It was well I knew nothing at the time about snakes shedding their skin or I'd have been worried, thinking this process might keep happening.

My father gave me a small, old, mahogany tabletop and a box of coloured chalks to keep me occupied. One day I was looking out the bedroom window, talking to some children on the street below, when they asked me for some of my chalk. I threw a few sticks down, but my father wouldn't let them pick them up. Handling my property might well expose them to the dangers of infection.

The next thing I remember seeing from the bedroom window was a car pulling up and a little white bundle being carried out of it and into the house. I knew this bundle contained my baby brother, Joseph. In due course, he and I became very close, as my mother, to all intents and purposes, made me his nanny. His birth and my scarlet fever are linked together in my memory.

One Sunday morning, almost three years later, my father said to me, in a strange sort of voice, 'Guess what we have, Molly.'

I stared, unable to imagine what could make him sound like that. He then said, 'A new baby.'

This was my sister, Alanna. My mother told me the nurse (a different one now: no longer Nurse Noonan) had found her in the country, near Brogan's Bridge. I believed her. My new baby sister had a barely visible, reddish mark on her shoulder.

After Mass, that same Sunday morning, I went up town and met some of the High Street children. The Power family said they had just got a baby boy. When I capped that with a baby girl no one believed me.

Alanna showed her ultra fastidious nature even in her cot. A nappy event had to be given immediate attention. As a toddler she couldn't bear to have a speck of dirt on herself or her clothes. But such a level of cleanliness was hard to achieve in our house.

Finally, Margo arrived. I came home from school one Thursday afternoon in September to find a big apple tart cooling on the bar counter. My father came downstairs and said the same thing in the same way as he had more than two years before. I knew at once what we had this time, but I was too wary to say it. However, he didn't keep me waiting and I rushed up to my mother's room. By then – I was nearly ten – I had somehow got to know the maternal part of the baby business. So I asked my mother if she was all right. 'Why wouldn't I be?' she answered, laughing.

Our family was now complete. Margo turned out to be a very outspoken child, often saying outrageous things the rest of us wouldn't even dare think. A few days after her birth, Catherine told me she'd known we were getting a new baby. A classmate of hers, Biddy Foy, had told her.

As a toddler, Margo had the painful distinction of being bitten by the seagull we found in the yard one snowy morning. We couldn't see anything wrong with it but it just wouldn't go away. Margo bent down to stroke it, saying 'Nicey birdie, nicey birdie.' Suddenly, it turned its head and jabbed her in the cheek, sending her indoors, howling. Eventually it took off.

It was Margo who thought of an explanation for Alanna's red spot. 'That was where God finished making her,' she said.

Looking back on our lives together, I feel glad I belonged to a fairly large family. I had a different relationship with each of my siblings. In *Mansfield Park*, Jane Austen comments on the unique nature of fraternal affection:

> Children of the same family, the same blood, with the same first associations and habits, have means of enjoyment in their power, which no subsequent connections can supply; and it must be by a long and unnatural estrangement... if such precious remains of the earliest attachments are ever entirely outlived.

We six certainly had that unique relationship and, although, to our deep grief, our brother died in his thirtieth year, these 'precious remains' still linger on between me and my sisters.

Notes

[5] Taoiseach: the title given to the Prime Minister of Ireland. It means 'Chieftain' in the Irish language.

[6] Irish Free State: In 1920, the British Parliament passed the Government of Ireland Act, partitioning the island. Six of the nine counties of Ulster (the northern province) accepted the Act. The rest of the country, the other twenty-six counties, rejected it. Fighting for complete independence from Britain broke out. In 1921, a Treaty with Britain allowed the twenty-six counties to become a self-governing country of the British Commonwealth. This was called the 'Irish Free State'.

[7] 'rotten' was no reflection on the condition of the orange, but was used indiscriminately as an expression of dislike. You might say it was the 'F word' of the day!

Doonbeg

Doonbeg

Think of a headless, lopsided rag doll, with a short neck, bloated top, tiny tum, floppy arms and legs, and you have it – the shape of Doonbeg, my home town in the west of Ireland. The neck is the High Street; the top, the Square; the tum, Middle Street; the arms Castle Road and Tannery Road; the legs, Church Road and Low Street with the knobbly knee of Air Hill. That's it.

Although this is how I see it in my mind's eye, according to geographical convention, it's upside down. The High Street actually points south.

Small as Doonbeg still is, it was even smaller in my time there – being as it was bare of the housing estates that now trim its edges.

The dot is the house where I was born: the second from the river on the Low Street and Tannery Road side of town. We liked to think we lived in the heart of things.

As Doonbeg children we felt the whole town belonged to us. We were street children in the sense that we felt free to roam around and play anywhere we liked. The Square was our main communal space. The children of the town had it to themselves, (except on Fair Days, of which there's more later.) It was a big, broad play area. On long, fine summer evenings we went through our repertoire of games there. We played catching, skipping, hopscotch, thread the needle, pussy in the well, round apple, the mulberry bush, and even the parlour game, blind man's buff. I don't suppose there's any play there now. The place is a car park, virtually.

Middle Street is where we 'lived, moved and had our being'[8]. We referred to the Square and the streets off it as 'up town'. There were four shops on our side of the street in those days. Neeson's was the corner shop, facing both our street and the Square. I remember old Mrs Neeson because she gave me a postcard of Shirley Temple. She thought I looked like her, but I had no idea who this child in the picture was.

Neeson's Archway separated the shop from the next two houses, which were sometimes in use, sometimes empty. Then came Hanrahan's house, then Tomeltey's, then Byrne's beside the river. Garvey's garden stretched behind our place and Mr Byrne's.

The eldest Hanrahan girl, Kitty, was Catherine's age; the second girl, Maureen, was about mine. She and I were good companions. The Hanley family, who lived on the opposite side of the street, gave us two more playmates. Dara was Catherine's age, and Peggy about mine. Peggy and I were regarded as partners in crime. She was judged to be the moving spirit, while I passed as the sleeping partner. But I think now it was a fairly equal pairing.

Our street – short and narrow – might have been aptly named Pub Row. Of the nine shops there then, seven were pubs. We were a pub, and we had a pub to the left of us, a pub to the right of us, a pub straight in front of us. Although each shop was a pub-cum-something, the pub was the main thing. We were bar and grocery; Neeson's was bar and drapery; Nugent's, opposite us, was bar and hardware.

Turning right at our shop door, going over the bridge and turning left, we came to Church Road. Here stood the church where we attended Mass and received the Sacraments. It was called St Finian's. For me, the highlight of the liturgical year was the Corpus Christi procession. Unusually, I was a flower-strewer for two years running; I was still small enough to look like a First Communicant, experienced enough to keep an eye on the others' baskets and replenish them from my large one, as required. We girls, dressed in our long, white Communion frocks and veils, each carried a decorated basket of rose petals which we scattered as we walked along before the Blessed Sacrament. The method was precise. You picked a petal from your basket, held it for a moment in front of you, kissed it and passed it over your shoulder. A teacher kept alongside the group, conducting *sotto voce*, so that we kept together, almost. The procession moved through every street, leaving a trail of petals in each one. Tubs of flowers on the pavement strengthened the scent that lingered all evening, mixed with the smell of incense used in the open air Benediction.

The Holy Week ceremonies, as we knew them, were very

impressive, even to a child. The church precinct is now a housing estate. A new church has been built on Dagoolan Road, just beyond the High Street.

Keeping to the right after passing the bridge brought you to Low Street, where we owned two tiny properties. I cannot call them cottages. They were simply one-room hovels with a back garden. In my earliest days one of them had a tenant who paid my father rent. Eventually they were knocked together to make, first, a turf-shed, and later, a garage. Finally, the site was sold to a neighbour and 'landscaped'.

Air Hill came into its own in icy weather. We had great fun sliding down it on our way home from school. The Old School, which we first went to, stood on the far side of Air Hill, at the very edge of town. The 'New' School stands on top of it.

Leaving the Square through the High Street, you come to the park, with the Town Hall squatting at its entrance like a gate-house. The park was one of my favourite places. Of course, it had no swings or contraptions of any kind. We devised our own amusements. From time to time, a tree came down in a storm. Then someone would put a board across it and we had a seesaw. Or we'd find a tree with an almost horizontal branch, tie a rope to it and make ourselves a swing. We climbed all the trees we could get a foothold on; played hide-and-seek among hillocks and hollows; ran around and sat about. I particularly liked a little grove of tall, straight trees with sparse grass beneath them. I thought there was something magical about the spot, the grass being so different there.

I loved the whole place in spring, when there were long banks of primroses everywhere, with some violets hidden among them. In autumn we delighted in the glossy horse chestnuts. We didn't call them conkers. This word was unknown in Doonbeg.

The park is now an adults' playground: it's become half a golf course.

Our river, the Dipper, was a great attraction. It had an odd reputation. It was said to thread itself under and over the ground in several places. I longed to find one of these places, but never did. How obliging of it, I thought, to make its own bridges. But perhaps the river only behaved like that in its formative years. We

Irish have such long memories: not just historical, but positively geological!

The main (man-made) bridge spans the river where it crosses the town, between our street and the little divide. We crossed the bridge going to and coming from school, and noticed the river's seasonal variations. Once or twice it overflowed into Mr Byrne's yard, and once it got into our kitchen. One summer it became a wadi.

Besides the bridge in town there was also the Barrack Bridge, a humpbacked, sorry piece of stonework. It was truly dilapidated: several stones had become loose over time and dropped into the water. A few of us would sometimes lie on the bridge, look through a hole and make hideous faces at the children below. When one looked up, those 'gargoyles' above made a weird spectacle. We reached it through the Barrack Square, the entrance to which was off Tannery Road. The Barrack itself, once the home of the Royal Irish Constabulary, was no longer there, having disappeared in the Troubles[9]. But the fascinating old bridge held out. In good summer weather it was the place to be. All the children of the town gathered there. We climbed over it, hung down from it, paddled under it, fished for *dearógs*[10] beside it. We squelched barefoot among the rushes, bulrushes and wild irises above and below it. Nobody fell though it. Long before now, the Safety Elf found and destroyed it. And Barrack Square has become a housing estate.

Doonbeg may not have been much of a town, but it was a paragon of a playground.

Notes

[8] This is from the New Testament, Acts 17:28.

[9] Troubles: We Irish believe our 'Troubles' began in 1169 with the Norman Invasion, and that they lasted with varying degrees of intensity down to the present time, although now that the Rev Ian Paisley and Mr Martin McGuinness are working together in Belfast and going on an American trip together, can we assume that our 'Troubles' are over? However, the particular aspect of the Troubles referred to here belongs to the 1920s. When the fighting for independence broke out, British army installations and government buildings were attacked. When the Irish Free State was set up, Civil War broke out because there were sharp divisions over the Treaty. It stopped in 1923 and the opposing factions became opposing political parties.

[10] *dearóg*: Irish word for 'minnow'.

Five Roads

We children of Doonbeg didn't confine ourselves to the Square and the six streets of the town, but went out into the surrounding countryside along each of the five roads out of it.

My mother took us for a walk on Sunday afternoons, weather permitting. We took straight walks and circular walks. Quite often we were a two-family, two-pram party when our next-door neighbour, Mrs Hanrahan, came too with some of her children. Turning left from our doorways into the Square, we had to decide which of the three roads to take. Castle Road, to our right, was a favourite. Naturally, it led to the Castle, the history of which has been fully documented, although that meant nothing to us children then. The Castle was simply the point at which the mothers turned the prams round and we all trooped back; or it was where they turned right to go 'round the bog', if they wanted a longer walk. It was, in fact, a walk through the bog. We came out on Church Road, arriving home from the right. Because that made it a circular walk, we called it going 'round the bog'. We also did that walk anticlockwise.

Another time, the mothers would go straight on through the High Street. This was a fairly short walk along the Dagoolan Road as far as the graveyard. But we added an extra stroll among the graves, with some reading of gravestones and prayers for the dead, and a look at the new digs.

The walk out of Tannery Road was quite long. When we'd passed the old tannery itself, long out of action, we kept going until we reached the traces of an old Ascendancy Estate[11]. It was here I first saw rhododendrons. We took our Christmas holly from this place. On very rare occasions we went even further, turning right to come out on the Dagoolan Road, well beyond the Graveyard. This made a very long circular walk. I don't remember ever doing this one in reverse.

The straight walk along Church Road took us to our Mountain: a ridge of some variety of sandstone, I believe. This reminds me that on a clear day – we had some – from various vantage points outside the town we could see the triangle of Croagh Patrick on the western horizon. We had many customers from the Mountain, all named Mulrooney. I once heard my father passing on a comment made by one of the Mulrooneys about the fifty acres of land he'd been given by the Irish Land Commission – '…two acres arable, forty-eight acres horrible.' The mountain walk was long. Sometimes we gave up and failed to get there, content to admire it from a distance.

When the mothers' choice of walk fell on Low Street, our walk in that direction, beyond Air Hill, took us to Beckett's Wood: a dark and fearsome place, it seemed, with a big old house glimpsed between the trees.

These, then, were the five furthest points we walked to along our five roads – the Castle, the Graveyard, the old Place, the Mountain and Beckett's Wood. We came to know every twist and turn, hill and hollow, bridge and brook along these stretches of road. We also knew who lived in every house we passed.

In time, of course, the pram parties ceased, but we older children visited these spots on our own, time and time again. They amounted to an extension of our town.

Notes

[11] Ascendancy Estate: At various points in the 16th and 17th centuries (from Mary Tudor in 1556 to Oliver Cromwell in 1654), the English government granted large tracts of land in Ireland to some of its chief supporters, who then came and settled on their Irish estates. Known, in time, as 'Anglo-Irish', these landowners became an aristocracy, while the indigenous population became the peasantry. Historians refer to this landowning class as the 'Protestant Ascendancy'. The perception is that they lived in grand houses, exacting as much rent as they could from their Catholic tenants who lived in miserable shanties. Eventually, resentment boiled over, leading to wholesale land reform, which began in the late 19th century.

The Way We Lived and What We Had

In 1910, when he was thirteen years old, my father came to Doonbeg from his mother's farm in Cloonlara – a district about twelve miles east of town. He came to be shop boy to his uncle, his mother's brother. After his uncle's death he bought the house and business from his uncle's widow. Or rather, his mother arranged a bank loan for him. The widow then went to live with other relatives in the country. My mother used to say they inveigled her, hoping for gain.

Anyway, as business remained notoriously bad throughout the thirties, my parents had an immense struggle to keep up the loan repayments, and to support themselves and us, as we kept coming. Catherine and I were all too aware of the situation and could see that we were less well off than many other families in the town.

However, in spite of the material difficulties, I'm sure we had all that really matters to children. Whenever I recall those early days I feel full of admiration for the single-minded way our parents concentrated on essentials.

We had our two parents, devoted to each other and to us. They were not outwardly affectionate, except to babies and toddlers. But we were completely at ease with them. We all took one another for granted. After all, family members have been granted to one another.

We had firm discipline. When a parent said 'no', no it was. It was a case of, 'no appeals, no conditions, no stays of execution, no compromises, no practical alternatives, final.' When I read this 'no' in Kingsley Amis' *The Old Devils*[12], I immediately recognised it as my father's 'no'. Absolute. Adamantine. Hard as it often seemed, we had to accept it. And it did mean we knew where we stood. We couldn't have a dog.

We had our parents with us always. As we lived over and behind the shop, neither of them left for work. I was in my tenth year before this pattern changed.

We had clear and simple guidance in matters of right and wrong. We were left in no doubt about the difference between good and bad, and about the need to try to be better. We soon learnt that bad behaviour brought bad consequences.

Our basic needs were adequately met. We were well fed, fairly well dressed and we had roaring turf fires to warm ourselves at. We were clean enough.

'What would you like?' was a question my mother never put to us about food. Dinner was dinner and that was that. If anyone demurred at anything her answer was, 'If you were hungry, you'd eat it.' We were and we did. I refused nothing. I was always the complete omnivore.

As my mother had to cook on the open fire, almost everything was boiled – mutton, bacon, cabbage, potatoes, root vegetables. Boiled mutton was the standard dish. But it certainly wasn't the '…eternal half-boiled leg of mutton, floating in a bloody sea of grease and gravy,' that Anthony Trollope complained so bitterly about[13]. It seems that's what was always served up to him on the Ballinasloe canal boats. Still, we were glad when something different unexpectedly came our way.

From time to time a customer or an aunt would bring us a fowl from their farm. It came in a canvas bag, fluttering and squawking. My mother got a local yardman to kill it. Customers might bring eggs or something as a thank-you gesture for credit. They might not be able to pay for their Christmas supplies until they sold some livestock at the following May Fair. Some might bring us a hunk of pork when they killed a pig. We sometimes bought rabbits from someone who snared them. On the rare occasion something in the 'gourmet' line appeared. I remember a wondrous pheasant and a salmon we were told to keep quiet about. We were once given a goose egg. Herrings were available on Fridays, and I recall a long ling[14] dangling outside a shop door in our own street. My mother may have bought a bit of it.

We helped our mother pluck the fowl and stood by while she gutted it. We also watched her skin and prepare the rabbit. Now and then she got an ox heart from the butcher. The stuffing that she put in it was better than the meat. I loved the black pudding she made with blood the butcher gave her for free. We ate liver, too. So, all in all, we had a certain amount of variety.

'Afters' were an occasional or seasonal treat, not an everyday course. We enjoyed rhubarb tart in summer, apple tart in autumn, apples and nuts at Hallowe'en, plum pudding at Christmas, and jelly and trifle now and then. Fruit, on the whole, was in short supply. An orange was normally sectioned among us. I still get a kick out of having a whole orange all to myself.

We had no sense of deprivation but were at times surprised when we came up against someone else's better standards. When a friend of Catherine's mentioned something about meat left over from the previous day's roast, I opened my eyes wide. Imagine having meat left over! The Christmas goose was the only thing not demolished in a sitting in our house. Then there was the green jelly, and the things that I thought looked like egg yolks, that we were offered at a neighbour's birthday party. When we told our mother about the green jelly we'd never seen before, she seemed hurt. 'That was lime or greengage,' she said. So I didn't like to mention the yellow things: tinned apricots I found out later. Lime jelly was served to us at home shortly after that, instead of the usual red.

Then there was the yellow satin episode. Peggy Hanley got a new dress of primrose satin with a white lace collar. I thought it was lovely. Then one Sunday Brenda Daley, from up town, looked it up and down, fingered the lace collar and grudgingly pronounced it 'nice'. Nice? Only nice? Surely it was the most beautiful dress in the world – in my part of it, anyway.

Our mother was our dressmaker and our father our cobbler. Of course the hand-me-down system was well used. On the morning of my Confirmation I saw a white object with a lace border hanging on the back of a chair. I didn't dare hope it was something new for me. It could be a pillowcase. My mother made pretty lace borders in crochet. They were used on many things. This, though, really was for me: a slip. What a delight! Notwith-standing my mother's talents as a seamstress, household linen must have been hard to maintain. The side-to-middle method gave sheets a new lease of life. It also gave them an uncomfortable seam. Cotton flour bags made good pillowcases.

We had some nasty things in our childhood. In her auto-biography Agatha Christie says she never saw a louse until, at the age of twenty-four, she nursed soldiers just back from the trenches of World War One. I didn't have to wait so long for my first sight of one. We all knew them from an early age.

Jane Austen, in one of her letters to her sister Cassandra, puts in a teasing message for their niece, 'little Cassie': 'If Cassandra fills my bed with fleas, I am sure they must bite herself.'[15] They certainly bit us.

And we had something nasty in the turf-shed – cockroaches[16]. Sometimes one unlucky one got into the turf bucket and ended up in the fire; then we heard it crackling as it shrivelled up.

Worst of all was the terrifying night Catherine and I woke up screaming. Something was scratching our faces. Our mother came running, and took us to her own room where she washed our cuts and put iodine on them. She said a cat had come down the chimney. We wondered where it had gone. Next day our father stuffed the holes in the skirting board with broken glass. Later we knew our attackers had been rats from the river.

We had plenty of fun in spite of some unpleasantness. In one of my last chats with my mother she stressed over and over again how much she had enjoyed all her babies. My father, too, was great at playing with little ones. He had a range of games with rhymes; a few in Irish. When Catherine and I saw him playing like that with the younger ones we knew he'd played with us in the same way, although we didn't remember it.

Our father loved to tell us about things we'd done and forgotten. It seems that a doll of mine had been missing for some time. When I happened to find it one day he asked me where the doll had been. 'In jail,' I replied.

'And why was the doll in jail, Molly?' he asked.

'Because she made a pee-pee in her knicks,' I said.

My father thought that was hilarious.

One incident that my father also thought funny, I do remember. It concerns a live present given to our neighbour. Just before Christmas one year, two ducks appeared in Mr Byrne's yard. My father said to me, 'Go upstairs Molly, and look out at the ducks waddling in Byrne's yard.'

'But ducks always waddle, Daddy,' I exclaimed.

'They don't always waddle this way, Molly,' said he.

So I went and looked. They were certainly waddling wonderfully well. Were they showing off? Then I noticed the brown frothy puddles dotted about. Mr Byrne must have thrown out some stale porter. The ducks were drunk. I wondered if that would make them taste better.

We children often had great fun among ourselves, although, to be sure, we quarrelled too. We probably helped to socialise one another. We played board games; draughts being a favourite. Our father would let his opponent win, as often as not. But sometimes, when we'd thought we'd won, he'd take three of four pieces in one go. It was all very good-humoured. Ludo, snakes and ladders and jigsaws came and went. If they'd come at Christmas they'd be gone by Epiphany. We weren't good at minding things. Draughts was the one durable.

Our father had a pack of cards as he liked to play with a few friends – who might also have a few drinks – late on a Sunday evening. No doubt 'after hours' made it more exciting. He let us have the pack every now and then. But we children only played Patience, Old Maid and Strip Jack.

We had a gramophone that was put on some Sundays, mostly wet ones. Records were of Irish dance music, Irish ballads, Percy French songs ('Are ye right there, Michael, are ye right?') and various tunes of the time. [17] My father was very fond of the song 'Isle of Capri'. When I heard it again, on the island itself a few years ago, it struck a resonant chord.

Notes

[12] *The Old Devils*: This novel by Kingsley Amis (1922–95) won the Booker Prize for fiction in 1986. The passage referred to is spoken by the character Muriel to her husband Peter. She is leaving him – 'checking out', as she puts it. Her mind is made up.

[13] Trollope quotation: The passage quoted is from the novel *The Kellys and the O'Kellys*, by Anthony Trollope (1815–82), who lived in Ireland almost continuously from 1841 until 1851. This was his second novel (1848), coming after *The Macdermots of Ballycloran* (1847). His work for the Post Office entailed much travelling so that he got to know the country and the people very well. He has written very movingly about the Great Famine of the mid-forties.

[14] 'ling' – 1) cod-like food fish (*molva molva*) of the North Atlantic; 2) Lake Ontario burbot (*lota maculosa*).

[15] Brian Wilks, Jane Austen, Galley Press, 1988, p.118.

[16] 'something nasty in the turf-shed': an allusion to 'something nasty in the woodshed', seen by the mad old character Ada Doom in *Cold Comfort Farm* (1932), by Stella Gibbons (1902–89). No one ever knows what the 'something nasty' was.

[17] Percy French: a famous Irish singer and songwriter (1854–1920). A landlord's son, he belonged to the 'Protestant Ascendancy', but that did not affect his popularity throughout the land. Many of his songs are comic. 'Are Ye Right There, Michael?' pokes fun at the West Clare Railway. 'The Mountains of Mourne' and 'Come Back, Paddy Reilly' are two of his best-known songs. There is a statue of him in Ballyjamesduff, Co. Cavan.

The Way We Lived and What We Hadn't

We hadn't any water. Drinking water or 'spring water', as we called it, had to be carried from the well on the edge of the town, opposite the old school. My father used to take me there with him. He carried the water in a white enamel bucket, which was guarded carefully when it reached home. We, and our clothes, were washed in rainwater, teemed from a barrel outside the back door.

The first improvement on this situation came when Timmy Nugent, the neighbour living opposite us, 'got the water in'. Good neighbour that he was, he allowed us access to it. We took it from the tap outside his kitchen door. There was no more going to the well. In time, to be sure, we 'got the water in' ourselves. It was a gradual process. The bar and the kitchen had sinks years before the waste room over the old stable became a bathroom.

One dry summer (there was at least one), the rainwater barrel was empty and my mother needed lots of tap water for the washing. So she kept me at home from school one day to fetch her enough from Timmy's tap. Can in hand, I crossed and re-crossed the road, over and back, time after time, until she'd had all she wanted. The handle of the can made grooves in my palms.

Shortly after this, the School Attendance Officer questioned all pupils absent since his last visit. I told him I was kept at home to help my mother.

'And what can you do?' he asked witheringly. I gave no answer.

When I told my mother about this later she said, 'You should have told him you could draw forty cans of water.' I thought she must have counted them.

We hadn't any 'cons'. (I say 'cons' because I want to avoid class-conscious, contentious, cloacal nomenclature.) I could tell you what we did but you wouldn't like it. Suffice it to say that there was an ash pit not many yards from the back door. But it wasn't just an ash pit. It doubled as a s— pit. (Although this pit-rhyming word and its fellows were unutterable and unprintable in those distant days, somehow we all knew them.)

Every now and then, when my mother could no longer stand the stench, she'd tell my father it was time to empty the ash pit. Then he'd borrow a donkey and cart, shovel the lot on and take it out to the street via Mr Byrne's yard, through which we had a right of way for this purpose only. There was a high stone wall with high metal gate in it between our two yards. The gate was opened only on these salubrious occasions. A robin used to wipe his beak across the top of this gate. It was a long time before I thought of asking where the donkey took his load. 'To the bog,' said my mother. Apt, wasn't it?

As with the state of our water supply, modernisation in this area also evolved slowly. Customers were served first. A 'what-you-may-call-it' appeared in a corner of the old stable, and later, in Garvey's garden – when we'd bought half of it – a male preserve was provided. A small area with a channel was walled off.

We hadn't any electricity in my earliest days. We used candles and oil lamps for our light. But it wasn't too long before we got wired up. To begin with, we had electric lighting on the ground floor only. I still went up to bed carrying my candlestick. Before the town was connected to the Shannon Scheme[18] we depended on a generator in a little powerhouse near the Park. I hated its thumping. And, in spite of its exertions, lights blinked and flickered, waxed and waned, and failed entirely at times.

We hadn't any pocket money throughout our childhood. That, I believe, applied to all the families we knew.

We hadn't any birthday presents, although the occasion was not altogether ignored. I did get a present on one memorable birthday, which I'll come to in due course. Santa Claus, then, was our only benefactor in the present line. We were always very happy with what he brought, but, as time went on, I couldn't help noticing how the children from the better-off families got the better presents. I thought that Santa should do it the other way round, bringing the best presents to the poorest children. I was surprised he didn't see it that way. Why didn't he bring the scooter to me instead of to Peggy Hanley?

We hadn't any money to spend at the carnival which came every year to the fair green. We might be given the price of one ride but we were lookers-on most of the time. I remember wandering around, looking at the 'Chair-O-Planes', flying boats, bumper cars and whatever else there was, wishing I could afford to try them all. It was at times like these we felt the pinch. However, we fared better when the circus put on its 'One Night Only' show in town. Our parents always found us sixpences for that. The value was wonderful. One saw the whole performance for one payment. Great, I thought. I wished I could do what the acrobats did. 'Tumblers', my father called them.

We hadn't any family holidays, ever. Even if we could have afforded to go anywhere, my parents wouldn't even consider shutting up shop and leaving for a few days. We had no days out, no meals out. Such things never crossed our minds.

We hadn't any business to speak of towards the end of the thirties. So my father had to take whatever scraps of casual work he could find. He took on the task of reading and recording the depth of the river for the County Council. It had to be done at regular intervals. A measuring post was fixed in the river bed, near the bridge. I often did the reading for him. I wondered why the Council wanted to know such a thing.

In the neutral Irish Free State, World War Two was referred to as the 'Emergency'. When this 'Emergency' began to cause shortages in some basic commodities it appears that the authorities aimed at achieving self-sufficiency, in sugar anyway. So an intensive publicity campaign exhorted farmers to 'Grow More Beet'. However, such a labour-intensive crop was not welcome in an area devoted mainly to meat production. Sugar factories got going though, and took men on for the winter months. My father did night work in Dagoolan factory for a few 'campaigns', as the periods of factory operations were called. He used to amuse our few bar customers with imitations of the accents of the foreign technicians employed there. Before long his own accent was to be ridiculed in another setting.

Our own business had now dwindled to almost zero. De Valera's reckless withholding of agreed payments to Britain led to predictable sanctions that brought calamity to Irish farmers, and to traders like my parents who depended on them. As my mother put it, there were days when no one darkened our door. I think the crisis point came towards the end of 1942. My father did what so many Irishmen did at that time; he found work in the 'Big Sister' island. For the rest of the war years, and for some time after, he worked on the railways, mainly in Swindon. Years later my mother told us that, when he left home, all the money they had was twelve pounds. So, for a few years, as so many Irish families did, we lived on an exile's remittances. With this money our living conditions improved noticeably. My mother must have been a good money manager.

One day, shortly after my father had left, I was at my usual listening post under the 'old' counter, when I overheard a conversation between my mother and another townswoman – one of the better off kind. She was telling my mother how 'great' she was to have let my father go.

'You have to chance things sometimes,' said my mother.

Then the woman began congratulating my mother on how well she was bringing us up. 'And they're all spotless,' she added, soulfully.

Not quite, I thought, looking down at my grubby, scabby knees. I didn't like the way this woman was talking to my mother. I'd have called it 'patronising' if I'd known the word.

Suddenly, out popped the insolent question: 'Do they each have their own toothbrush?'

There was the slightest hesitation before the answer came.

'Musha,[19] no, they don't,' replied my mother.

I was delighted she'd told the truth, knowing as I did that there wasn't a truthbrush – I mean toothbrush – in the house at the time. It doesn't seem to have mattered much, however. I still have twenty-eight sound teeth.

A year later I, too, left home. So there was our house sadly depleted: no Daddy, no toothbrush, no Molly. November?[20]

Notes

[18] The Shannon Scheme: The Shannon, Ireland's largest river, rises in Co. Cavan, not far from the border of Northern Ireland, and flows into the Atlantic Ocean near Limerick. In the mid 1920s the Irish Free State employed a German firm to build a giant hydro-electric power station, using the waters of the Shannon. It was duly built at Ardnacrusha, a few miles north of Limerick city. Known as 'the Shannon Scheme', it powered the national grid and enabled rural electrification to take place.

[19] 'Musha' is an introductory word used in Ireland, commonly used to give the speaker time to think – the same as saying 'Um… you know…'

[20] 'November?': The poem 'NO!' by Thomas Hood (1799–1945) came to mind. It begins 'No sun, no moon, no morn, no noon,' and carries on in that vein, ending with 'No fruits, no flowers, no leaves, no birds – November!'

The Old School

Take off your coats,
All you who enter here,
And shiver all day,
In cold and fear.

I exaggerate of course, but the Old School really wasn't a comfortable place, in any sense of the word, for either teachers or pupils. It was an open-plan, boot-shaped enclosure. Three teachers worked in it, in full sight and sound of one another. Miss McGinty had the calf, Miss Hanrahan the heel, Mrs O'Donahue the toe. Each teacher's section was called a Division, although there were no physical partitions. Miss McGinty taught the Infants, aged four to six. Mrs O'Donahue had the Middle Division, aged seven to nine. Miss Hanrahan taught the Seniors, aged ten to twelve, or older. Some pupils remained at Primary School until they reached the school leaving of fourteen. The total number of girls would have been between a hundred and a hundred and ten.

Hold out your hand! The command echoes down the years. Slapping was an integral part of the system. However, I have no recollection of Miss McGinty slapping anyone. Maybe it was felt that at those tender years we were still 'trailing clouds of glory'[21] and therefore untouchable. Or maybe it was simply Miss McGinty's own tender heart. The business got underway, though, in the Middle Division.

We had different ways of complying with the order. Cliona Ryan raised her arm above shoulder height. Then her palm had to be pressed down, none too gently, to a manageable level. Afterwards she squeezed the affected palm in her armpit. I always felt sorry for Biddy Tierney who had very slender fingers, the little one of which invariably separated from the others and somehow, almost always, got a touch of the cane. I put out a reluctant forearm, keeping my elbow clamped to my side. Our hands tingled for a little while, but it was the indignity we felt most. Told it was for our own good, we took it in our stride.

Miss Hanrahan's nieces, Kitty and Maureen, however, got it in the neck. This was not at all because of failure at lessons or persistently bad behaviour. It was only because both Mrs O'Donahue and Miss Hanrahan had advanced views. They must have been the first practitioners of political correctness in the western world. Nobody would be able to accuse them of favouritism, nepotism or any other -ism. They leaned over backwards to prove that consanguinity didn't count with them. (We all knew that word. It was one of the impediments to Matrimony.) So Kitty and Maureen were not spared.

Situated well apart from the school itself was a separate little construction. Let's call it the Orion Block[22]. If houses and shops could do without 'cons', it was agreed that the school could not. This facility was set up at the back of the playground, facing the low stone wall that separated the school from the Canon's field. It 'consisted of' (we used that phrase a lot in our compositions) three compartments. The first, the teachers', had a door and a bolt. The other two had rickety doors, sometimes. So the almost Roman, open-plan arrangement offered a golden career opportunity to an aspiring peeping Tom. What a good thing the Canon wasn't one.

My clearest memory of the 'cons' is of a new girl sitting there, wearing a bottle green dress in a material I'd never noticed before. When I described it to my mother after school she said it was corduroy. I had another reason for remembering this girl. She had her knickers down round her ankles. The rest of us used a different method. We didn't go so far. Cultural differences are remarkably noteworthy. I won't give this girl's name, as I don't suppose anyone would like to know that she remains stuck forever in someone's memory in such a situation. Her initials give us Elsie.

In the summer holidays Miss Hanrahan got John Maughan to do something about the Orion Block. John was a very tall, very thin tinker. I don't know if John's modus operandi was the same as my father's. Whatever he did, when we came back in September the place smelled of lime. It made a difference.

The adjacent boys' school was much the same, I imagine. I never set foot in it.

Notes

[21] 'trailing clouds of glory': This is a quotation from 'Ode on Intimations of Immortality from Recollections of Early Childhood' by Wordsworth. It appeared in *Poems in Two Volumes* in 1807.

[22] Orion Block: In Greek mythology many different stories are told of Orion, the hunter. There are two versions of his name: 'Orion', meaning 'mountain-dweller', and 'Urion', meaning 'he who makes water'. As the son of Poseidon, the water-god, he obviously had rain-making powers, the constellation Orion being associated with rainfall.

Miss McGinty's

I tried to start school in September 1936. Because Catherine went to school I thought I should go too. But, as I was still under four years of age, Miss Hanrahan couldn't enrol me and sent me home again. I remember that event well. I was wearing a pale green dress my mother had knitted me. However, I have no recollection at all of the day I really began.

My clearest memory of my time at Miss McGinty's concerns the sound of music. She used to give us little ear tests, three or four notes at a time. She hummed, or went la-la. Then you had to tell her the sol-fa names of the notes. It might be soh, mi, soh, doh: I couldn't understand how she expected us to know what she was thinking of. That's what it seemed like to me. I never knew. What puzzled me most was the fact that the same two girls always got it right. To my mind, neither of these two 'never knew nothing'. Excuse my Spanish. You get my meaning. How on earth could they do something I couldn't? Long after I knew the answer to that, I was pleased to find I erred in good company when I read Charles Lamb's rhyme about his own powers of musical appreciation:

> Some cry up Haydn, some Mozart,
> As the whim bites. For my part,
> I do not give a farthing candle
> For either of them, nor for Handel.[23]

Unlike Lamb, though, I'm not quite tone-deaf. I mean I can tell 'The Last Rose of Summer' from 'The Yellow Rose of Texas' from 'Mexicali Rose from 'The Rose of Tralee' or a rose by any other name. Whoa! I'm gathering too many roses. I'm getting carried away. Nevertheless, I can't confidently distinguish between a major and a minor third. So I never got the hang of Miss McGinty's humming and hawing. It was definitely not 'so me'.

An interesting feature of the Infant Division was the Gallery. This was a flight of wooden steps leading to a wide platform on which stood a shrine to Our Lady. There was a ball frame[24] there too. Only the High Infants were allowed on the Gallery. So I thought that's why they were called High Infants. I recalled that little misunderstanding of mine on reading of Laurie Lee's disappointment at not getting the 'present' his teacher had seemed to promise him when she told him to 'sit there for the present'[25].

I still feel guilty about something I did in Miss McGinty's. Sitting next to me was a child I didn't like because she had a runny nose. This particular day she had a horrid, green and yellow, thick, wormy thing dangling from it. She dropped her pencil, and when she got to the floor under the bench by my feet, I kicked her in the mouth. She cannot have made much of a fuss, as there was no investigation. I felt wretched at once. I suppose I'd have felt better if I hadn't got away with it. Remembering this, years later, I thought I knew how Jane Austen's Emma felt when Mr Knightley reprimanded her for her treatment of Miss Bates at the picnic on Box Hill.

Miss McGinty, thinking I could read the clock, sent me once to Miss Hanrahan's to find out the time. Obediently I went and looked, knowing it didn't mean a thing to me. I went back, having decided to take a chance. I'd have a bet on it.

'A hundred to eight,' I said.

I'd heard my father say this most distinctly in the course of a story he'd been telling at the bar. Still, like most bets, it didn't come off. The teacher gave me a funny look and sent someone else.

I was off sick when they started 'carrying' in subtraction. My father was overseeing my homework the evening of the day I went back. In one sum, when he didn't mention this funny business, I reminded him, 'You have to do something,' I said.

'Not in this one,' he said. So you didn't have to do it every time. But how could you tell?

All things considered, my time in the Infant Division seemed full of puzzles.

I thought Miss McGinty wore lovely jumper suits.

Notes

[23] Lamb quotation: from *Verse and Worse: A Private Collection* by Arnold Silcock, Faber and Faber Ltd, 1952.

[24] Ball frame: abacus.

[25] Laurie Lee (1914–97): The reference is to Lee's best-known work, *Cider with Rosie* (1959), a memoir of his Gloucestershire childhood.

Lysheen

My father's sister, Aunt Molly, and her husband, Danny, had no children. When they offered to bring me up, my parents considered it. Already, in 1938, they had four children. As business was so bad they were struggling to make ends meet. So I was asked if I'd like to go and live with Aunt Molly. I said I would. I went off with her very happily. I don't know when exactly I went but I know I was there for my sixth birthday in October.

My aunt and uncle lived on a farm by the sea in a 'townland'[26] called Lysheen, two counties away. It was a totally new environment for me. I remember next to nothing about the school, except that I went in the company of two big girls, neighbours of ours, who minded me going and coming. It was a long walk.

I have only two memories of the few months I spent at my aunt's that year. The first concerns my uncle's mother who lived with us. Although they assured me she was not sick, she stayed in bed all the time, even during the day. I couldn't understand why. I didn't like going into her room, as there was always a soggy newspaper mat beside her bed and a bad smell all round. But, the day after my birthday, I couldn't resist showing off my fine, new baby doll.

'Where did you get that doll?' she asked me.

'My mother sent it to me,' I answered.

'You're a liar,' said she. 'You told me yesterday that the postman had given it to you.'

I knew there was something wrong with her conclusion but felt unable to argue the point.

'You're a smelly old woman,' I said, 'and my doll hates you.'

So that visit was over.

My second clear memory also concerns a relative of Uncle Danny, a distant cousin this time, Kitty Mulanney who was reputed to have certain healing powers. She had 'the cure'. After a short visit she'd paid us one day, my aunt asked her to mind me for an hour or so at her own house. We set off across the fields. On the way, Nature called and Kitty squatted. She was a very fat lady. So what I found myself staring at next comes to mind now as a giant white peach. At that time I'd never heard of a peach of any size or colour, but that's what that big bare bottom looked like.

'What are you looking at?' The gruff voice startled me. I had no answer to that. What indeed? The odd thing is that she got her revenge five years later. Let me get back to you on that.

My parents took me home at Christmas. They were sorry they'd let me go. But, if I was as quiet as they kept saying I was, I'm surprised they missed me!

When I returned to Miss McGinty's in the New Year I found a new puzzle before me on the blackboard. The day's date was always there at the top, in three sets of figures. The first two sets changed but the third had always been '38' for as long as I could remember. Now it was '39'. What did that mean?

In July I moved up into the Middle Division. In those days our school year began on the first of July, a few weeks before the summer holidays.

Notes

[26] Irish usage, meaning a division of land of various sizes.

How I Became an Example of Boldness

This episode is my most poignant memory of my time in the Old School. I should say, perhaps, that we were not 'naughty' in Ireland. We were 'bold'. In this case, though, 'bold' is really the better word.

It was sewing time in Mrs O'Donahue's and I was having terrible trouble with my stitching. It just wouldn't come right. Time and time again I took it to the teacher's table for inspection, and time and time again she sent me back to undo and repeat the thing. The scrap of lawn was getting dirtier and dirtier, and I was getting crosser and crosser. Then I pricked my finger and a big blob of blood fell on the stuff.

'You needn't shed your blood over it, Molly,' said Mrs O'Donahue, the next time she looked. I could take no more.

'I'm going to tell my mother about you when I go home,' I retorted. 'And I'm going now,' I added, defiantly. So up I got and out I ran. No one tried to stop me, even as I rushed through Miss Hanrahan's section.

No doubt there was consternation at home over my untimely arrival with my tale of woe. But my parents must have realised how distressed I was, as I was not even scolded. Nor was any reference made to the matter at school next day, nor at any other time. I suppose it was such an unprecedented thing that no one knew what to do about it. Years later my mother told me that because of it a coolness had arisen between them and the school; the reason being, as she put it, that '...we didn't go down on our knees to apologise to them.'

My only reprimand came from one of Miss Hanrahan's pupils, a classmate of Catherine. She said, 'Molly Tomeltey, you were an example of boldness the day you ran out of school.'

The words came from behind me as I walked along the High Street, some months after the event. I turned round. My accuser was Brigid Madden, a fairly new girl whose father had come to work in the bank. She certainly had no right to say such a thing to me, I felt. However, I said nothing; just turned back and kept going.

Nonetheless her cutting remark brought the painful happening to my mind in full force.

Ghost Words

I call them ghost words because each of them haunted me for a time and still seem like little characters that played a part in my life.

The first was the combination 'octoberdicktobin'. The day I was told my birthday was in October a customer called Dick Tobin came in to the shop. At once the two names flew to each other and became a chant that went on in my head for several days. It was hard to shake off.

When I had a 'bird disease' called thrush I had to rinse my mouth with deep purple liquid, called, my father told me, permanganate of potash or potassium permanganate. That, too, banged on at me for days. I don't know which bothered me the most – the disease or the cure. That particular phantom pounced on me again when I came across 'purple-stained mouth' in my poetry book some years later.

After that I had a sore foot which was treated with putty-like poultice, described as 'antiphlogistic'. That word was one more to be reckoned with. But it never popped up again. It faded away as the foot got better.

'Nasturtium' was an early ghost word of mine, and a naughty imp it was too. One lunchtime, as I was leaving school to go home for my midday meal, Annie Cox, who lived nearby, collared me and gave me sixpence to buy her a packet of nasturtium seeds in Timmy Nugent's shop. She of course knew that I lived opposite him. Not having heard the word 'nasturtium' before, I realised I had to nurture it carefully as I went along. So I kept repeating it to myself. However, in spite of all my efforts, something happened to it as I crossed the bridge. Like Tam O'Shanter's mare[27], it was curtailed. Then I feared that the defective version might not pass muster. People might laugh. It was a funny word anyway, however you said it. I took my usual route, the line of least resistance. I crossed the road, ate my dinner and went back to Annie Cox.

'He hadn't any,' I said. She looked surprised but said nothing.

By this time the crows were cawing above the playground, quarrelling over crusts. That meant the children had gone in. I was late. Oddly enough, I didn't get told off. All three teachers were toasting their shins at Miss Hanrahan's fire.

After such a troublesome introduction to Nasturtiums I've never liked the golden goblins.

The name 'Aloysius' haunted me around Confirmation time, when we were deciding what names to take. I'd come across it in my prayer book and regarded it as an old friend that answered to the sound. 'Alloy-See-Us'. But when I heard someone call it 'Aloe-Wish-Us' I went off it. How could a word, a Saint's name at that, play such a trick on one? I chose Alphonsus instead. In any case, this was the name my mother had taken for her Confirmation.

Ennis or Venice? I knew Ennis was a town in County Clare, and Venice a city in Italy. But which of them did the Merchant come from? These were twin ghosts. My mother finally laid them to rest for me.

'Lamb's Tales from Shakespeare' came to my ears as 'lambs' tails'. What could it mean? In addition to his poaching activities did Shakespeare go around docking lambs' tails? Did he pass them round to his classmates? 'I got a lamb's tail from Shakespeare. Did you?'

When I heard that a boy from up town had got a 'Scholar Ship', I was totally nonplussed. I kept thinking of it as a sailing ship, although I suspected it couldn't be any kind of real ship. So what was it?

All of my ghost words still have, for me, a hazy aura of the magic that once surrounded them.

Notes

[27] Tam O'Shanter's mare: A reference to 'Tam O'Shanter', a narrative poem by Robert Burns (1759–96). One night, the hero, Tam, was riding home from the tavern on his mare, Meg, when he caught sight of a band of witches and wizards having a dance. Greatly taken with the performance of one young witch, who was wearing a 'cutty sark' (short shift or mini-dress), Tam had to show his appreciation:

> Tam tint his reason a' thegither,
> And roars out 'Weel done, Cutty sark!'
> And in an instant all was dark!

That was his mistake. Maddened by the interruption, these frightful creatures went after Tam and Meg like a swarm of angry bees. Tam knew they would be safe once they'd reached the cornerstone of the bridge, as evil spirits could not cross running water. Meg got Tam to safety but didn't quite make it herself. 'Cutty Sark', at the head of the troupe, grabbed Meg's tail and yanked most of it off.

> Ae spring brought off her master hale
> But left behind her ain grey tail.
> The carlin claught her by the rump,
> And left poor Maggie scarce a stump.

Mrs O'Donahue's

My memories of the Middle Division are mainly of Multiplication Tables, Catechism and Irish Grammar.

Unlike the learners of today, we had an infinite variety of Tables with a vocabulary one rarely met again. We used a wide range of numbers from four 'gills' or 'naggins' in one pint; up to 4840 square yards in one acre – and, it seemed, nearly every number in between. In the Multiplication Tables we didn't just learn the answer. We had to tag on the answer in shillings and pence as well. We had the table of Length from inches to miles, to leagues indeed. And that list even had a half in it: five and a half yards in one perch, pole or rod. Then the square measure of that had a quarter in it. It was tough going! We learned two tables of Weight – Troy and Avoirdupois. I liked the former which began with 24 grains in one pennyweight. We had Liquid measure and Dry measure. The last item in 'Dry' was rather odd. It said five quarters in one load. Load of what, I wondered? Was it all really necessary?

As it was in Arithmetic, so it was in Catechism. Rote-learning loomed large. The principle seemed to be: memorise now, understand later. But what do I do as I wait for understanding to come? I play with my wonderful words and phrases and apply my own meaning to them. I tended to follow Carroll's Humpty Dumpty's way with words – 'When I use a word it means just what I choose it to mean.' For one thing, the instruction to our First Parents to 'increase and multiply and fill the earth', gave me much food for thought. 'Increase' was something my mother did in her knitting. 'Decrease' was another thing, but that didn't come into this. 'Multiply' took us back to the top of the page with sums. Curious. 'Fill the earth'? Surely, it's full already. It's not hollow like that trick Easter egg that was such a let down; all dolled up and as empty as a balloon, when I thought I was getting a solid ball of chocolate. What would they fill the earth with, anyway?

Could there possibly be a mistake in the book and it should be 'till' the earth?

There were many lists in the Catechism, of good things and of bad. There were the Seven Deadly Sins, the Seven Corporal Works of Mercy, the Seven Spiritual Works of Mercy, and many other Sevens. My favourite set was what I now call the Big Four – the four sins that cry to Heaven for vengeance. The first was wilful murder. Yes, I saw there could be no question about that. Next came the sin of Sodom. Now who was he? And what did he do? (We never heard of the one he was twinned with. Remember we didn't read the Bible. We read a 'judicious' selection of Bible stories.) The corruption of the innocent was third on the list. To me, this meant a little boy with a pus-y thumb. Where was the sin? Defrauding the labourer of his wages was the fourth one. My mother committed that. She never paid Willy Reilly when he killed a hen for us.

I think one of these Four has been deselected lately; or perhaps just downgraded.

Our Bible storybook was illustrated, but the only picture I remember clearly is 'The Miraculous Draught of Fishes'. It stuck in my mind for two reasons. First, 'draught' in its liquid form meant draught Guinness. What was the word doing here? I knew Our Lord had turned water into wine at the wedding of Cana. But I'd never heard he'd turned the lake of Genesaret into porter. Secondly, the Archangel Raphael painted this picture. His name was beneath it.

'Cat' or 'cant'? *Requiescat in pace* or *Requiescant in pace*? Spot the difference. It took me more than one funeral to work it out.

Having three age groups to juggle with, no teacher could possibly keep us all on task all the time. So I found myself a nice little occupation to fill in spare moments when I'd finished the set work. Taking a pencil in each hand, I started writing with both hands, in contrary motion, beginning in the middle of the page. The jotter I used was narrow, so pages filled up fairly fast as I got better at it. But I didn't dare use my wide exercise book. At home, I'd hold the work up to a mirror to see how the left hand bit had come out. I kept the practice up until it palled. I was never caught.

A rather unkind routine was carried out over books and fuel.

Parents had to pay for these things, and many couldn't easily afford to. At the beginning of the new school year the textbooks were handed out. Then, from time to time, enquiries were made and the money asked for.

'Stand up those that haven't yet paid for their books,' Mrs O'Donahue would say. I was often among the number that stood up.

'I can't understand how anyone would begrudge you money for books,' she said to me on one occasion. 'You make such good use of them.'

A compliment with a sting in its head? I knew well my parents didn't begrudge me money for books. They simply hadn't it.

There was limited provision of free books which I had at times. They bore a label inside the front cover, telling you whose property they were. I remember just one sentence from it – 'If it is lost or torn it must be replaced or paid for.' But I have no memory of any follow up of either kind. Maybe they were never lost or torn.

As for fuel, some pupils brought turf, some brought money. As my father always gave a cartload of turf, I was never in the firing line on the days the fuel was asked for.

Although we must have spent a lot of time reading and writing in English and Irish, I cannot recall much of the matters we dealt with. I wasn't a bad speller, so I felt ashamed of myself one day when I found I had written 'rember' for 'remember'. Bananas had gone off the market by that time, so that I couldn't have made a slip up in that one. (If banana comes to mind, can slip be far behind?) I didn't know 'queue'.

I wrote a short 'composition' about Muldoon's Alsatian, Conor – the best known dog in town. Unfortunately for them both, he bit Dara Hanley and had to go.

In spite of the sewing episode and the book money business, I was quite happy in the Middle Division. Mrs O'Donahue slapped our palms often, but lightly. I could live with it. She was forever threatening to hit someone's head against the wainscoting. She never did, though. On the whole, I got on well with her and she sometimes used me as a kind of monitor. She might, on occasion, entrust me with the answer book to mark sums. She shouldn't have! I sometimes yielded to entreaty and would mark a wrong sum right, especially if they were *all* wrong. A tick for effort might be granted. An early example of an examiner dumbing down?

One morning I came in late to find her already at the board, going over Irish irregular verbs with one group. Without a word she handed me the pointer, indicating I was to take her place while she moved over to another group. She needed whatever help she could get.

It was during these years that my various escapades round the town took place. But the order of events is not noted in my book of memory.

Some of My Sins

I messed up my first Confession. When I came out of the box I turned round to leave the church and go home. Someone grabbed me and pulled me back.

'You have to say your penance,' she said.

'I've said it,' I insisted. 'I said it in the box.'

'You're not supposed to do that,' she said. 'You go to a seat and say it there.' (We never said 'pew').

I went to a seat. Feeling all eyes on me, I said my prescribed three Hail Marys again. Perhaps I thought the first three were null and void, for technical reasons. I mustn't have been listening in class when we were told the bit about the seat. I must have been doing that woolgathering Mrs O'Donahue was forever accusing me of.

Sometimes a customer would give me a penny, out of the goodness of their heart – and their shallow pocket. One great red-letter day I got a threepenny bit. Straight away, I rushed to Doran's on Tannery Road to buy a penny packet[28]. I was hoping to find a doll in it; a tiny Bakelite doll made in Japan. Dolls were the only toys I cared for. There wasn't one in every packet. This time I was lucky. When I handed over the threepenny bit, Eileen Doran gave me back five halfpenny pieces instead of four. I took them, knowing I shouldn't. When I got home I displayed my change in great glee. But my father made me go back and return the extra halfpenny. Eileen accepted it.

Mrs McGonigal, who had a small sweet shop on Castle Road, wanted some help with her household tasks and in the shop. So she asked my mother for me and I got the job. It seems I did the domestic work to her entire satisfaction, as I was soon promoted to the commercial side. First, it was simply a matter of standing behind the counter and calling her when someone came in. It was during these minding times that temptation came. Alone among sweets and chocolates, I ate some. They were not immediately missed, so I was allowed to go on to the next stage – actually serving people. However, like Eileen Doran, I had problems with change. One day, two customers bought a few items that came to either one and fourpence or one and twopence – I forget which. They gave me half-a-crown. It took me so long to work out the change that one of them said in a loud whisper, 'She doesn't know what change to give.' Nonetheless, they accepted whatever I gave them and left.

Of course, before too long, Mrs McGonigal realised she had a staff theft problem and terminated my contract. Because of my difficulties with change I was glad to go. She cannot have told on me to my mother, as there was no mention of the matter at home. So ended my short career as a shop girl.

The next sin that comes to mind is similar; but the setting was entirely domestic and I had an accomplice. The Hanrahans' garret on the second floor was a single large area where we often played with the Hanrahan children. It would have made a fine artist's studio I imagine. One day Maureen and I, after a long period of play in the garret, went down to the parlour on the first floor. Set out on a small table near the piano was a large plate of fancy biscuits. A siphon of soda water stood by. Maureen said all this was for her aunts – the teachers – who lodged with them at the time. It was an enticing selection of biscuits: iced ones in pink, lemon and chocolate, some white fluffy ones and jam puffs – Jacob's best. Two would not be missed, we thought. Maybe four. Even six. And so it went on. We were like Carroll's Walrus and Carpenter[29]. We left them the soda water; it got up our noses.

Of course there were repercussions. Mr Hanrahan punished Maureen, but the guest delinquent was granted immunity.

Shortly after this the aunts moved into a house of their own on Air Hill, almost opposite the New School. While Miss Eileen was Principal of the Girl's half, Miss Becky had to bike it to a country school. Maureen and I believed that we'd brought this move about. Post quod and all that. Knowing there was little love lost between Mrs Hanrahan and the aunts, we wondered if she was secretly pleased with us.

I have a hazy memory of us two eating ham sandwiches in Hanrahan's on a Friday, another time. We'd forgotten it was Friday, so no guilt was attached to that.

I had another accomplice in my next piece of wrongdoing. Peggy Hanley and I decided to vandalise the O'Donahues' garden when we knew they'd gone to the seaside for a week in the summer holidays. In the event, though, we didn't do a thorough job. We got cold feet once we got in there. So we just beheaded a few big yellow flowers.

I don't think we deliberately gunned for teachers! We simply used the opportunities that came our way.

Knock-and-Run was a common antisocial antic among us. There wasn't enormous scope for it, as there were few private houses, and the owners were usually at their shops when we were on the prowl. Where there was a maid she always know somehow that it was 'only kids' and wouldn't bother to answer the door. The most productive places were the bank and Mr Bodkin's, both in Tannery Road. Mr Swan, the bank caretaker, would pounce and growl. Mr Bodkin, an old man, would come after us with a bone-handled knife and a loud roar. It was great fun. I think he enjoyed it as much as we. Some years later, when I first came on the words 'bare bodkin'[30] in a play I needn't name, the image they conjured up for me was that of a naked Mr Bodkin b(e)aring down on us. Was that a bread knife that I saw behind me?[31] (The play that actors dare not name also came to mind.) The Bank is still there, although Mr Bodkin has long since made his quietus.

In the family I was considered truthful. However, I did lie to my mother once. I forget what about.

'Are you telling me a lie?' she asked.

'I am,' I said. That settled that.

I missed Mass one New Year's Day, which was, in those days, a Holy Day of Obligation. It was the feast of the Circumcision – that meant it was the day on which Our Lord was given his Holy Name. As my parents were busy in the shop, I was minding some of the younger ones. It was only when the Church bell rang that my mother realised I was still in the house.

'You should be gone to Mass by now, Molly,' she said. So off I went. But when I reached the Church door I found it blocked by a crowd of men. Too timid to try and make my way through the throng, I turned round and went home again. I managed to slip in unnoticed. Now that sin of omission has lain on my conscience all these years! I mustn't have confessed it!

To finish – as we finish sacramental Confession – 'that's all, as far as I can remember.'

Notes

[28] Penny packet: a square or rhomboid sachet of thin card, covered with coloured paper, containing a variety of tiny toys and knick-knacks rather like those found today in cheap Christmas crackers. As the name implies, it cost a penny.

[29] The Walrus and the Carpenter: This nonsense poem by Lewis Carroll (1832–98) is found in *Through the Looking Glass and What Alice Found There*, published in 1871. The poem is recited to Alice by Tweedledee. The Walrus and the Carpenter invited the young oysters for a walk along the beach. Unsuspecting, they accepted. After a mile or so the hosts settled on a rock and ate every one of their guests.

[30] 'bare bodkin': refers to Shakespeare's *Hamlet*, Act III, Scene 1. It is from his most famous soliloquy, 'To be or not to be':

> For who would bear the whips and scorns of time
>
> …
>
> When he himself might his quietus make
> With a bare bodkin?

[31] Bread-knife: a disrespectful allusion to *Macbeth*! Act II, Scene 1:

> Is this a dagger which I see before me?

Sixty of the Best

Still in Mrs O'Donahue's, I watched this performance in fearful fascination from a safe distance. It was Geography time in Miss Hanrahan's. The sixth class were supposed to have learned something about the fruit crops grown around Naples. That had been their homework. They were expected to have memorised the relevant passage in the textbook. Miss Hanrahan asked for the list.

'Oranges,' someone offered. The rest were silent. Miss Hanrahan waited. Oranges were not the only fruit. Even then. There were also lemons, figs and dates. Miss Hanrahan proceeded to hammer the message home. She unhooked the cane from the wall and the class lined up. They got four wallops each, to match the list. Miss Hanrahan called out the items as she delivered the blows, slap and fruit combined. It went like this:

> Right hand, *swish*, oranges.
> Left hand, *swish*, lemons.
> Right hand, *swish*, figs.
> Left hand, *swish*, dates.

The action was repeated until the entire class of fifteen had received their punishment – and the message. Even I, an uninvolved bystander, got the message, and never forgot it. I watched to see if the contributor of 'oranges' was let off one whack. But no, she got the full course of treatment. The rhythm could not be broken. For as Miss Hanrahan caned away, she swayed from side to side, getting redder and hotter.

I was then eight or so and knew that as soon as I got into double figures I'd be for the Senior Division. But I wasn't unduly worried. I might be dead by then.

Miss Hanrahan's teaching was vigorous, if not rigorous.

Scarred for Life

Of course we knew there was a war on but thought it hadn't anything to do with us. It was brought home to us, however, in a number of small ways.

The most exciting thing was the news of the alien who had landed by parachute in a field ten or so miles away. All who could visited the scene. Those of us who couldn't had to be content with scraps of white silk that were handed around the town, and said to be bits of parachute. We heard that the alien had been arrested and never heard another word about him.

Then the doctor's family had a refugee boy staying with them for some time. His name sounded to me like 'High Mow'. As something rather exotic he was lionised by the boys of the town.

There was food rationing at some stage. But I think it was quite like Fasting and Abstinence in the Church today – barely there.

Now, rightly or wrongly, when a number of trees were cut down in the Park, I believed it had something to do with the war. Perhaps timber was in short supply. Anyway, the day I found about twenty tree trunks lying neatly on the grass, parallel to one another, just my long-jump distance apart, naturally I had to jump from one to another. I got through the first course without mishap. It was on the return journey that I became a casualty of war. I lost my footing and pitched forward. Then a sharp, vicious little twig gouged a scoop of flesh out of my leg.

Some years ago, on a television programme, Clement Freud was asked what he thought was the first thing people noticed about him. He said it was the scar on the inside of his left thigh. Now if that wasn't a memorable reply in itself, it was memorable to me because I have a scar on the outside of my right thigh. But it's not as eye-catching as the Freudian one.

As I dripped slowly home I left a trickle of blood on the High Street, like the one that came there on visiting dentist day. When my father saw my gaping gash he rushed across the road to fetch Jimmy Nugent, Timmy's brother, a chemist who happened to be home on holiday. Jimmy bound up my wound, pouring in a good splash of iodine. Doctor Baker might have wanted twopence, maybe more.

'Molly,' said my father, 'you'll have the mark of this until your dying day.'

I took that to mean that on that day it would go.

So the morning I wake up to find it gone I'll know that Birnam Wood has come to Dunsinane.[32]

Notes

[32] Birnam Wood has come to Dunsinane: The allusion is to *Macbeth*, Act IV, Scene i. The Third Apparition speaks to Macbeth:

> Macbeth shall never vanquished be until
> Great Birnam Wood to high Dunsinane hill
> Shall come against him.

Trying for a Baby

Peggy Hanley's mother was a widow at this time. But that didn't stop some 'slithy toves'[33] from up town from urging Peggy to harass her mother to get a baby. She did her best, all to no avail. Pester power was not so potent in those days. So Peggy and I decided to take matters into our own hands.

If Mrs Noonan could find babies, so could we. We searched as many gardens as we could get into, including our patch in Low Street. We looked under heads of cabbage, the prime site. We examined shrubs and bushes, scanned flowerbeds. There wasn't a cry or a stir anywhere. We were getting more and more disheartened. Then I had an idea: a Biblical one.

'Peggy,' said I, 'we'll go to the river and try that place where the bulrushes are.'

I liked those bulrushes. They had tops like fingers in brown suede gloves. I wished I had some brown suede gloves. Anyway, we went to the river bank, but our search was equally fruitless. The bulrushes were no better than the gardens. Maybe, after all, it was only people like Mrs Noonan who could find a baby.

Said my mother, years later, 'Wouldn't it have been fun if you'd found one?'

Notes

[33] 'Slithy toves': The phrase is from the first line of 'Jabberwocky', the poem in mirror-writing that Alice found on a table in *Through the Looking Glass*. Later, Humpty Dumpty explained the first verse to her, saying 'slithy' meant 'lithe and slimy' and 'toves' could take many forms. So, with his permission, I use 'toves' here to mean 'smart alecs'.

Hanley's Back

This was one of the Middle Street children's favourite haunts. It was a big, high-ceilinged, barn-like annex behind the shop. It had probably been a warehouse or a storeroom in Victorian times. Hanley's hall door fanlight bore the date 1829, the year of O'Connell[34] as every Irish man, woman and child knows – or used to know. Anyway, the Back was now used only as a play area, except in the month of July.

We played school, shop, house and church. School was mostly scolding and caning. Shop was bargaining. If it was a draper's the customer would try everything on, keep finding fault and buy nothing. Our favourite game was house. Lacking 'proper' toys, we improvised and dramatised. As Dara put it to me some years ago, we had to use our imaginations. Old boards became house walls, internal and external. Cardboard boxes became pieces of furniture. We used shards of broken crockery, glass jars, tins, the foil lining from tea chests, scraps of cellophane – in short, whatever we could find. We were wombles before the Wombles. Sweet wrappers were made into thimble-sized cups for dolls' tea sets. We had dolls, always, if nothing else.

We played dentist and patient, occasionally, whenever something reminded someone of that scene. This was a grimace and spit act.

We liked to give ourselves high-sounding names. For some length of time I was Emma Mount Severn, while Kitty Hanrahan was Mrs Great Southern.[35] I'd have swapped with her had I known then that I was destined to marry the Anorak of Anoraks![36]

On the rare occasion when there was a boy among us we did Mass or Benediction. The celebrant invented a language of his own as he went along. An authentic Latin phrase rang out at intervals. As we all knew the responses to *Dominus Vobiscum* and *Orate Fratres*, we listened for them. The part we knew best was the Greek *Kyrie*, because of the repetition no doubt.

In summer, after the sheep shearing, huge bags of wool were piled high in Hanley's Back. It was a wonderful opportunity to take the high jump of your life. You chose a high pile, with an unfinished one beside it. Then you climbed to the top of the high one, your head touching the ceiling. You jumped, knowing you were sure of a safe, if bouncy, landing. I did it, over and over again. It was the most exciting thing in Doonbeg. It was miles ahead of the Chair-O-Planes, bumpers or anything else the Carnival could offer on its annual visits. I still thrill to recall the sensation. I think of it as skydiving in miniature.

Outside the Back proper there was a narrow passage where we played in summer. It led from the yard of a nearby pub out to Castle Road. Known as the Dardanelles, it was used as an escape route by after-hours drinkers. Sometimes a customer would forget to buy Guard O'Ecks his regular double Jameson. When that happened the guard would remember the licensing laws and a stampede for the Dardanelles would follow. Of course, we children knew of no other Dardanelles. This was the Dardanelles, pure and simple. I thought the name just right for a place with so much fuchsia sprawling all over it.

I thought I'd made a mouse friend once in the Dardanelles. I spotted it sitting on a crate of bottles, grooming itself. When I looked at it, it looked at me, briefly interrupting its task. I got on with my own occupation. Neither of us minded the other. Then I had to go home to my lunch. How disappointed I felt on my return to find the mouse gone.

Notes

[34] O'Connell: Daniel O'Connell (1775–1847) is known in Irish history as the 'Liberator' because of his struggle to gain civil rights for Catholics and for the prominent part he played in getting the Catholic Emancipation Act passed by the British Parliament in 1829. Then in 1840 he founded the Repeal Association after which the agitation to end the Union with Britain gained momentum.

[35] Emma Mount Severn was a character in the romantic, much-dramatised novel *East Lynne* by Mrs Henry Wood (1814–87). Her most successful work, it appeared in 1861. Mrs Great Southern was a name Kitty got from Great Southern Railway – a 'going concern' at the time.

[36] My husband has been an inveterate rail buff since his teens. A much-travelled man, he is well-known in railway circles as a photographer and writer. As he has been referred to in a recent article as 'that legendary enthusiast', I feel wholly justified in dubbing him the 'Anorak of Anoraks'. Nowadays, though, he's more the Columbo Mac!

Fair Day

I don't mean swings and roundabouts. I mean pigs, cattle, sheep and horses; mostly sheep. The Fair was held on two consecutive days each month. Pigs had the first day all to themselves, the other animals got the second. It was on different dates every month. My father knew them all but I had to look them up in Old Moore's Almanac. I have since wondered how the fairs of Doonbeg came to be listed in a book of astrology, first published in 1700, under the title *Vox Stellarum*. My mother only remembered the date of the May fair for that was the date she felt my first feeble flutter. She told me that, long afterwards, when it was safe to do so.

The pigs were confined to the Square, as was most of the extra trade they brought with them. My mother resented this. It meant we had to rely heavily on the second day. The great thing about that second day was the fact that the school was closed. As the streets were stuffed with farm animals, even a cat couldn't have got through unscathed. Preparations for the big day began on pig fair evening.

'Timmy, don't forget to tap the half-barrel,' my mother used to say. I wondered why it was called a half-barrel. It was a whole barrel really and bigger than the firkin we usually had on tap. Of course, when I got to the full range of the Capacity Tables in Mrs O'Donahue's Division, all was revealed. In the meantime the half-barrel remained an enigma.

On fair morning our parents had an exemption. This meant they got up in the dark to open the shop, and let in some of the sheep there wasn't enough room for on the street. You've heard of the pig in the parlour. Well, we had the sheep in the shop. They pressed in, wethers and hoggets and all. Some farmers came in also, and a dog or two.

My mother sent us upstairs for the day and got Dolly Mul-rooney from the Mountain to keep us there. She came in for that purpose the evening before. She generally managed to prevent us from invading the ground floor, going down to the kitchen herself from time to time to pick up provisions for us. On Fair days the kitchen doubled up as a lounge bar for women and old men.

Catherine and I always went down at least once. Each of us had a pet old man that we simply had to see. Both had nicknames. Hers was called Snug. Mine was Culk. Although Snug was our father's Uncle Michael, like everyone else we never called him anything but Snug; or in exact Doonbeg mode – Schnug. He brought his jennet to town with him on Fair days. Now, this jennet, being family, got much further than the sheep. He was led right through the shop, into the kitchen, across to the back door, down the yard and into the old stable where he remained tethered for the day, without the least sign of restiveness. He was within easy reach of his nosebag of oats or hay.

As soon as Catherine realised Snug had come, she rushed down in great excitement, shouting 'Schnug and the jennet, Schnug and the jennet.' The other old man, Culk, was a great friend of mine. I don't know how it came about, but everyone accepted that each of us was the other's favourite. He was eighty. I was eight. Love is certainly a mystery!

Although Dolly fulfilled her main function of keeping us out of the way, she was less successful at keeping us out of mischief. We pulled down curtains and curtain poles to make tents and wigwams. We made igloos from sheets. We raided our mother's precious remnants tea chest to dress up in a crazy patchwork of colour. We made trampolines of the beds. We pulled the horse-hair out of the old furniture in the waste room over the old stable. This room was a dangerous place, with stacks of old stuff and holes in the floor. However, nothing we did there had to be accounted for. The jennet below never reacted to the sporadic commotion overhead.

Before she left, Dolly tried to restore the status quo in the other rooms, but we still had to face the music of our mother's anger the next day.

By late afternoon both we and the Fair were subsiding. Soon all the bargaining, barking, bleating, bellowing, lowing, braying and neighing had died away. Then Dolly played a game with us, when she finally got us to sit down. She made us sit in a row with our legs straight out. The game was played to the accompaniment of the zaniest rhyme one ever heard:

> Oorel, awrel, umble, ock,
> Five miles at ten o'clock,
> I sat in the sun,
> I rarely spun
> A little white dog
> At the mountain's butt,
> And for that same reason –
> Put in that FOOT.

As she recited it, she touched a foot at each stressed syllable. The foot touched at the word 'FOOT' had to be pulled back, and was then 'out'. The game went on until we were all 'footless', whereupon we hastily put our shoes on, ran downstairs and out into the street, to join the other 'footless' ones.

Middle Street was now a thoroughfare once more, no longer a corral. The sheep and cattle had left for fresh woods and pastures new[37] – and badly they needed them at this time of day. Unlike the street sweeper they didn't wait for tomorrow. Naturally, the circles they left behind craved wary walking[38]. You had to find the gap.

Now, if reading maketh a full man[39], Guinness maketh an overflowing man. And at this time on Fair evening the farmers were full, the half-barrels were empty and the lack of 'cons' began to make itself felt. Had a 'Good Loo Guide to Doonbeg' been issued at that time, Neeson's Archway would have been *numero uno* – and *numero dos* too, I fear.

So we scuttled through this Archway, trying to catch a glimpse. But drunk as they were, the men were ultra careful. They were no flashers. They merely shook a fist at us. As a result, our failure rate was high; sightings were rare – as rare as mushrooms in August in Macauley's field.

We went through to Garvey's garden where we hung about for a bit. Then, like the Wise Men, we went back home another way.

Notes

[37] Fresh woods and pastures new: The allusion is to the elegy 'Lycidas' by John Milton (1608–74). The poem ends with the lines:

> At last he rose, and twitch'd his Mantle blue:
> To morrow to fresh Woods and Pastures new.

[38] Craved wary walking: A quotation from Shakespeare's Julius Caesar, Act II, Scene i:

> It is the bright day that brings forth the adder,
> And that craves wary walking.

[39] 'reading maketh a full man': This is from the essay 'Of Studies' by Francis Bacon (1561–1626).

> Reading maketh a full man, conference a ready man and writing an exact man.

Sneak Preview

Just as I had had a brief preview of the Old School in 1936, so I had a sneak preview of the new one in 1940. Although nearly finished at the time, it was still a building site. But the order KEEP OUT – writ however large – wasn't enough to stop me and Peggy Hanley from looking the place over for ourselves. The flimsy fencing round it was no barrier to us. We got in easily.

How different it was from the school we knew. It was one long piece, half for girls, half for boys. We kept to our own half, knowing the other would be the same.

We got in at one end and found ourselves at the head of a long passage. 'That's called a corridor,' my mother told me afterwards. We started walking through it. Doors off this passage took us into rooms, one for each teacher, it seemed. How strange. Then I noticed a rubber knob on a wall behind a door. Wondering what it was for, I banged the door a few time against it. I knew then. The knob stuck fast.

Next we found the most fascinating thing about the whole place. This was the row of six lovely, little, low lavatories. We'd seen these white items before, in a big, old, empty house on the Castle Road. Those were dry, but each of these school ones had a pool of water in it. Peggy knew what to do about that. So we flushed them all. The pools wouldn't go away, though, however often we tried to get rid of them. Each lavatory had SHANKS CARDIFF printed on it. What could that mean? I thought it very funny that the walls between them reached neither floor nor ceiling. Very odd.

Then we found a little extra room at the top of a few stone steps. We were so absorbed in our tour of inspection that we didn't notice the passage of time. The general rule was that we always had to head for home as soon as we heard the six o'clock Angelus bell. That evening it didn't ring for us and we got back inexcusably late.

When my father heard where I'd been he gave me the whacking of my life. It was like the one he gave Catherine the day she took the half-crown out of the till. I had weals on my legs for days.

No doubt, some super-sensitive child protection people would be horrified at this. But what are a few red marks on the sturdy limbs of a healthy eight year old – fresh from a blatant bout of delinquency – compared with the daily Dunblanes the Scots Archbishop lately referred to?

I admit I did feel resentful at the time, yet not so much because I'd been beaten, but because Peggy Hanley hadn't. Mothers didn't beat, although our mother held the wooden spoon over us as a sort of sword of Damocles[40]. A reminder of its existence served.

Notes

[40] Damocles: Legend has it that Damocles was a courtier of the elder Dionysius, ruler of Syracuse (405–367 BC). Because Damocles envied royalty, Dionysius decided to teach him a lesson. He invited him to a great feast but placed over his head a sharp sword hanging only by a single horsehair. 'Uneasy lies the head that wears the crown' was the lesson for Damocles.

The New School

I was still in Mrs O'Donahue's when we moved into the New School in 1940. I was impressed by the green-topped desks we had in the classrooms; they were so different from our old benches. Mrs O'Donahue got us to draw a plan of our new classroom. She went to some length explaining what was meant by a plan, in that sense. I liked my plan, probably the only one I've ever done. I kept it by me for some time.

In due course I moved up into the Senior Division and was relieved to find it was not at all the terrible place I had dreaded in the past. Indeed we seemed to have moved into calmer waters generally in the new school. An occasional squall developed, to be sure, but the sailing was smooth enough.

Once again, sewing-class memories surface first. I have pleasant images of Miss Hanrahan teaching me how to sew on a button and to do both buttonhole stitch and its near relation, blanket stitch. In one of these I had to put the thread round the needle. In the other it did the job itself, if I held it the right way. Then there were patches and gussets. I managed the patches, but botched the gussets. We did darning too.

In knitting we did heel-turning and toe-narrowing. I was glad to be let off the full sock. Grafting was the grand finale of the toe job. Miss Hanrahan had a code for it. It went: up and off, down and on, down and off, up and on. Or vice versa. Or something. The ups and downs referred to the directions the needle was pointed in. The ons and offs told one when to leave the stitch on the needle and when to knock it off. The process went on and on until the toe hole healed over – or caved in completely. It came to an end somehow.

In geography, lists persisted. A few have stayed with me, such as these Scandinavian sea channels: the Skagerrak, the Kattegat, the Sound, the Great Belt and the Little Belt. Once I'd got over the first two, the rest was downhill. Actually, one of these two did me a favour recently. When we were watching University Challenge it meant that I knew a geographical fact my husband didn't. This bears out the old adage: 'Keep a thing; its use will come.' I also hold a little list of rivers in Sweden. I looked them up the other day to see if they were really there. They were, in a slightly different form, the atlas having gone all linguistically correct. But they were still recognisably my old sitting tenants. It's time they earned their keep.

We had a little book of English grammar. It took a no-nonsense approach. It began boldly with its definition of a noun, something like 'A noun is the name of any person, place, or thing, action or idea of the mind, as James, Dublin, book, writing, joy.' Perhaps it's time this sort of thing made a comeback!

Miss Hanrahan was a stickler for the distinction between 'can' and 'may'. A nice little exchange on this point took place one day between her and me.

'Can I open the window, Miss?' I asked.

'Well, I really don't know, Molly,' she said very sweetly. We smiled at each other and I tried again.

'May I open the window, Miss?' I asked.

'Certainly you may, Molly,' she replied.

That surprised me as I thought she was going to refuse. I must have been fonder of fresh air then than I am now.

I remember standing by her side at her table, as she filled in my Confirmation card. When I gave the name Alphonsus she repeated it softly to herself, pausing after each syllable, using thumb and three fingers to help out. That action alerted me. So I watched to see if she spelled it correctly. (Insufferable child.) She did.

A regular visitor to Miss Hanrahan's was a tall, red-haired, blue-eyed inspector. Those eyes were like the bluestone we had in the shop in summer. The farmers bought it to make a spray to protect the potato crop from blight or something. It was a lovely colour but we were absolutely forbidden to touch it. It was copper sulphate, I think. Miss Hanrahan had to raise her head and stretch her neck to look into those bluestone eyes. I've never seen any others like them!

My time in the Senior Division came to an abrupt end. When

we broke up for the Christmas holidays, 1943, I'd no idea I'd not
be going back in the New Year.

Jobs for Mammy

We didn't do chores. We did jobs. And we were required to do quite a few. I was happy enough with most of them, although I hated being called on out of the blue when I was deeply engrossed in something of my own. A few tasks I found a little irksome.

We had jobs to do in the house, errands to run round the town and forays into the country. As we got older we realised, of course, that our mother couldn't do everything herself, unaided.

I was my brother's minder. But I didn't mind him very well the time I let him fall off my mother's bed. The thud and the scream brought her bounding up from the shop. She was so concerned for him that she never uttered a word of reproach to me, careless as I'd been. However, Joseph was perfectly all right, apart from a bump and a bruise that soon showed up.

As I was with him when he took his first few independent steps, I was under the impression that I'd taught him to walk. I quite enjoyed minding him, except when one of the neighbouring girls came to ask me out to play. Then I dodged him and slipped off. There was a lengthy period during which I had to stay by his cot every evening until he fell asleep. I told him stories and recited all the nursery rhymes I knew. At some point I carried out my awake-or-asleep test. I started singing (my way) 'Come Back, Paddy Reilly, to Ballyjamesduff.' If he didn't join in he was asleep and I could blow the candle out and leave. If he did join in, I had to stay. Sometimes, though, I'd be sneaking out when I'd be the one to get called back. Then the whole rigmarole had to be repeated.

I was my mother's wool-minder or, to be fair to the others, one of her wool-minders. I can't remember when the old counter became the wool counter, but at some point my mother rescued it and set up a wool department there, getting her supplies from Dwyer's of Cork. She knitted a few sample jumpers and pullovers which were promptly bought up, so that she had to knit some more. Then people kept giving her orders until she had more than she could deal with. In time, she got a machine which speeded production greatly. Sales grew. Eventually, Dwyer's told her that she was their best knitting wool customer. Indeed, in the early years of the war, when the rest of our business had almost ceased to function, my mother's wool department was our lifeline.

In those days yarn came to the shops in big hanks, not in neat, needle-ready balls, as it does today. We children often had the tiresome task of holding out our arms to support the hank and keep it fairly taut while our mother wound it into a ball. Soon, two of us did it for her, one holding, the other winding, then reversing roles for the next hank. To spare our arms, we some-times placed two chairs back to back, a suitable distance apart, and put the hank round them. But it kept slipping down.

In time we were able to help our mother with the knitting itself, working basques and cuffs, so that she could begin the pattern and shaping straight away. She became known in the parish as a 'great knitter'. We girls became fair knitters – Alanna an expert one – and we have kept it up. It was time-consuming work but I think our mother found it paid. After all, she needed every shilling she could make.

I did my share of the daily round of washing-up, sweeping, dusting, tidying, bed-making and keeping the kitchen fire going. As regards the latter, though, I have to say that I hear now an accusing chorus of sister voices saying: 'You were always letting the fire go out.' I also helped with the weekly, occasional and seasonal jobs. A weekly task was polishing the linoleum flooring upstairs. I rather liked that. I could slide around on the floor cloth, once I'd rubbed the polish in. But I sometimes stubbed a toe against the wall by not braking in time. I was considered a good floor polisher. As well as the process, I liked the end result too – a glossy mirror-like surface. Window cleaning gave similar satisfaction.

I wondered why the egg spoons got special attention. They were the only things we cleaned with bath brick. I was reminded of this stuff when I saw a piece of it recently in Beamish Open Air Museum. It was a friable block that we scraped with a knife. Then we wet the powder and cleaned the spoons with the resulting paste.

Pounding the blankets was a summer job we enjoyed. First, we had to wash our feet, as we might have been going about barefoot. Then my mother put hot, soapy water in the washtub and dropped one or two blankets into it. Our job was to jump in and dance about on them, pounding them down into the water. We had to do it one by one, the tub being a little one. I found that when I pushed a bit of blanket down in one spot it bubbled up in another and had to be pounded on again. It was fun, whether effective or not. My mother told us they did something like that with grapes in foreign countries. (I believe mechanisation has now changed all that, the old way still used only by the Symington family in one of their places in Portugal.) It occurred to me that we could do it with blackberries. Imagine being up to one's knees in blackberry mush. What could we do next to make wine of it?

My mother rarely visited any other shop in town. We children shopped for the commodities we didn't stock ourselves. We went to the butcher, the Post Office and the Medical Hall which was our name for the chemist. Whenever my mother wanted something in the drapery line we would go and get several items for her to choose from, three or four dresses or blouses or hats or whatever. The task often entailed visits to each of the four drapers we had and several trips to and fro. If she wanted a length of material they would give us tiny cuts off several rolls. When one suited her we'd go back with the order. One summer everyone was buying light stuff called 'Sparva'.

We also had to go for the milk. Our supplier always added a 'supeen' for the cat, whether the customer had one or not.

In late summer and early autumn we were sent into the country to pick blackberries and crab apples for jelly. I loved blackberry-ing. I ate as I picked. It didn't bother me to think that spiders and other types may well have been scuttling all over them before I get there. Few of us had the self-control to wait until the fruit had been washed. And even now I eat them straight off the bramble. Every year I was intrigued anew by the way the unlikely crab apples were made into jelly. I watched the pot to see the yellowish juice become a beautiful shade of red, as it came to the boil. Where did that mysterious colour come from? During the 'Emergency' extra 'sugar for jam' was available.

We were sent into the country on other errands also. We often went to collect homemade butter which my mother had arranged to buy from a farmer's wife. We called it country butter and we all preferred it to the creamery variety sold in the shops. As well as the butter, the farmer's wife, as often as not, would give us free buttermilk, which my mother used in bread making. Sometimes we were given an additional present – rhubarb perhaps – or a few apples. Once I was given an enormous marrow that I was barely able to carry home. Someone I met on the way teased me, saying it was bigger than me.

Some of this may sound something like child labour but actually much of it was a pleasant mixture of work and play. We still had ample time for pure play.

The only job I really hated was washing the potatoes in the morning before going to school.

Jobs for Daddy

'Dropping the corks' was the main job we had to do for our father. He bottled about six dozen half-pints of Guinness at a time. When they were all filled to the neck with good, brown stout and lined up on the counter in neat, regimental order, he dragged the corking machine out of its corner and called one of us to drop the corks for him.

He placed the bottle on a little circular platform above which was the little well we dropped the cork into. Something held it there until our father worked the handle of the machine. Then the cork was squeezed and pressed down into the bottle. Now he wasn't a very patient man and he worked the handle hard and fast. It was entirely up to us to get our finger out of the way before it got the squeeze too. Inevitably, we weren't always quick enough. So, from time to time, one or other of us would sport a black spot under or on the nail of an index finger. We would keep an eye on it until it grew out. Sometimes the black spot fell off half way up the nail. This was an integral hazard of the job.

After the bottling came the labelling. Labels were oval in shape, buff in colour, with the Guinness name writ large, and 'Bottled by Vendor' writ small. We used size to make paste to stick them on with. My father did most of the labelling himself, afraid, with good reason, that we might make a mess of it.

Occasionally, we helped with the bottle washing. We used lead shot for that. We put a handful of it in the bottle with a little water and shook and shook, mouth of bottle held firmly against the palm. Then, when we hoped it was clean we poured the shot into another one and rinsed the first out. We returned them to their correct crate to dry.

Sometimes our father trusted Catherine and me to wash the glasses unsupervised. First we emptied all the dregs into one pint glass. Never too fastidious, each of us took a mouthful of the mixture before throwing it away. When we'd washed the glasses we left them to dry, upside down on a pitted white enamel drainer which rested on a tray which took the drips. I don't suppose we got a sparkling result.

Footing the turf was the other big job I helped my father with. We did this work in the bog. It was not, let me assure you, the bog the donkey and cart went to. The bog we got our turf from was much further away, close to my father's mother's place.

As we didn't own a stretch of bog ourselves, our father had to rent a bank every season. A bank was like a little cliff out of the face of which the sods of turf were cut. After cutting came the scattering. I was never present for these first two stages. It was at the third stage, the footing, that I came in.

Footing meant making *grógeens* which, in turn, meant little stool-like arrangements of sods. Three or four sods were made to stand on end, supporting one another like drinking pals. One or two sods were placed across the top, making the seat of the stool. This was considered the best way to dry them out. It was, to be sure, always fine in the bog: we only went there on fine days.

Clamping followed footing. Clamps were small ricks – a pile of peat bricks stacked against each other to dry. Finally, when thoroughly dry, the turf was ricked. It then waited to be carted away at a convenient time.

My father kept an old kettle and an old saucepan in a clump of heather throughout the turf saving season. He left tea and sugar there too. At lunchtime he made a fire. Then he made tea in the kettle and boiled eggs in the saucepan. I was amazed to see him do these things here in the bog when he never did anything like that in the kitchen at home. When all was ready we had our picnic.

It was a pleasant interlude in a fragrant place. Besides furze and heather there was bog cotton with its fluffy, white heads nodding in the breeze. Tiny flowers grew all around. They seemed to be such weak little wisps, in pallid shades of pink and lilac that when I was told later that some of them trapped and ate insects, I was taken aback. Still, as my mother would say, if you find yourself in a bad stand you have to take advantage of any passing traffic. I never knew these flowers' names.

Here and there were mounds of brilliant green, mossy stuff, like emerald velvet cushions. But my father warned me against them. If I stepped on one I might find it was resting on water. Deep water. A bog hole, in fact.

We went to and from the bog on my father's bike. Sometimes I sat on the crossbar in front of him, sometimes on a makeshift seat tied to the carrier behind him. Neither perch was comfortable. The crossbar, even side-saddle, was severe on the fundament. The back seat had its own drawback. My father insisted I keep my legs well clear of the wheel, in case my skirt got tangled in the spokes and sent us both flying. So I had to freeze in a leap-frog pose for the ten mile journey, each way.

This bog job only lasted a season or two. I got too big and heavy to be transported in this way! Anyway, eventually, my father himself said goodbye to all that backbreaking work and bought a lorry load of Bordnamona machine-cut turf.

Nothing to Read

We all liked reading, as soon as we got the hang of it. But we couldn't get enough of it – literally. We had no school library, no town library and there were very few books in the house. We couldn't afford them. So we had to make do with whatever stray odds and ends came our way.

In the shop, besides the two working counters, the bar and the grocery, there was the old counter under which some huge tomes lurked. You know the un-put-down-able. We had the un-lift-up-able, in the shape of old Victorian ledgers which must have been well over a foot high. There they lay, among yellow newspapers, brown spittoons and towers of invoices on spikes. Naturally, one left them where they were but it was possible to turn over the pages. I thought the writing was beautiful and the entries astonishing. Items such as 'Side of Bacon 3*s*.4*d*, Firkin of Stout 1*s*.9*d*.' made the mind boggle. Great Uncle Thomas must have done business on a bigger scale than we did. And no wonder; everything was so cheap!

Then there was a tattered old dictionary, back cover missing. There was a medical book, the most interesting of these heavies. It had fearsome illustrations of the pop-up kind. One of these showed a man 'turned inside out', as Bernadette put it.

My mother had a four-volume set of Alban Butler's *Lives of the Fathers, Martyrs and other Saints*[41]. The pedlar who sold it to her must have been a great salesman. For a few years she managed to protect the work from us, only allowing us to look at it on a Sunday when she was free to watch over it. But eventually she gave up and the books fell apart. I felt a pang of nostalgia recently when I came across a rather similar edition of the work in a second-hand bookshop in Brighton.

There were only two 'proper' books in the house. One was *Trent's Last Case*, the other Jane Austen's *Pride and Prejudice*. I began both.

I stopped reading the first when I realised the end was missing. Someone had pulled out the last few leaves. For years I thought of it as unfinished business. When I found a whole copy of it in 1990 I began it again and finished it this time.

Pride and Prejudice, Everyman Edition, had a sort of promise at the beginning, saying it was '…a tale which holdeth children from play and old men from the chimney corner.' It was many a year before I found out that this was a quotation from Sir Philip Sidney. Relying on this promise, I started hopefully. Soon, however, I decided it wouldn't hold this child from play and indeed the old men could stay in the chimney corner while they read it, if they wanted to.

That Mrs Bennett began to annoy me. Why did she keep calling her husband Mr Bennett? No woman I knew called her husband 'Mr'. I had been interested in her at first, because, like my mother, she had five daughters. But, unlike us, they had no brother. I got the idea that if they'd had a brother, they could have stayed at home and not gone out to get their feet wet looking for a rich man to marry. I left them to it and took a rain check. Had I but known!

Santa Claus brought a few books and we managed to borrow a few from our neighbours from time to time. Somehow we got to know some Aesop, Andersen and the Grimms. But we never heard of Kenneth Grahame or A A Milne. Timmy Nugent, who lived opposite us, supplied the school with textbooks and stationery. He also had a collection of old storybooks in a storeroom behind the shop. He let me borrow them. I remember his *Jason and the Golden Fleece* and a few Arabian Nights. I think it was from him too that I got *Androcles and the Lion* which my father read to me[42]. What a wonderful ending that story had! 'It was the same lion,' I breathed. I was so impressed that ever after I kept a lookout for that lion. And, of course, he kept, and keeps, appearing. Storytellers cannot do without him.

Although there were no Victorian novels in the house, my father knew something of the works of Dickens, Thackeray and Eliot. I never heard him mention Trollope. I find this surprising, considering the years Trollope spent in Ireland, and the Irish elements in his work. His first two novels were set in Ireland to which milieu he returned in *The Land Leaguers* in the eleventh hour of his career. He also gave the Irish character Phineas Finn a substantial role in the *Palliser* series. Trollope may well have passed our door time and time again when he was travelling in the vicinity.

My father knew something, too, of some eighteenth century writers: Defoe, Swift, Goldsmith. He went to school in Doonbeg for one year, finishing his formal education at fourteen.

I cannot recall seeing any book of verse in the house but my father liked the poems of James Clarence Mangan. He taught me two of them, 'Dark Rosaleen' and 'The Woman of Three Cows', both translations from Irish. He recited them from memory. I also picked up from him a little of 'The Nameless One'. He also taught me a bit of Goldsmith's 'Deserted Village'.

The only verse I heard from my mother was one she said they used to chant at her school, at the other end of the county. Its theme was geographical. It went:

> Dublin on the Liffey,
> Cork on the Lee,
> Limerick on the Shannon,
> And the master on the Spree.

Of course, in those pre-Beijing/Mumbai days, 'Spree' rhymed with 'Lee'.[43] I'm told that nowadays it rhymes with 'Lay'.

Peggy Hanley got the *Dandy* and the *Beano* regularly and was kind enough to pass them on to me. I loved them.

My mother bought a woman's magazine occasionally. *Rebecca* and *One Pair of Hands* were serialised in it. I may have read bits of both at the time, although I generally avoided serials. As my mother didn't get the magazine every week I thought it would be like doing a jigsaw with just a few scattered pieces. I read a few short stories but found them disappointing and gave them up. I became familiar with the name 'Barbara Cartland' printed in stylish lettering. I heard of *Gone with the Wind* and *The Wizard of Oz*. Having tried everything else, I started taking an interest in the advertisements. Soon it was being said in the family that I only read advertisements.

There was a recurring one I found very puzzling. The woman in the picture was said to have five days more to live or sometimes just three. Yet she was shown riding her bicycle and laughing her head off. How could she? I knew death was no laughing matter. When a little girl in town died of 'new monia' everybody cried behind her small, white coffin. But then I thought of something that happened when Miss Coyle, Mr Byrne's aunt, died next door to us. The empty coffin had been carried upstairs to receive the corpse, but it was then decided to let the full coffin down through a window – the narrow, winding stairs having been deemed unfit for purpose. So a steep ramp of planks was placed under the chosen window. Joseph and I watched the proceedings from our adjacent window, sash raised to give as a better view.

'If these men are not more careful, they'll kill poor Miss Coyle,' called Joseph in a loud voice. I could see the men trying and failing to hold their laughter. So there could be fun at a funeral. I half thought myself that the jolting might have a Snow White effect and that Miss Coyle might lift the lid and sit up.

Anyway, I asked my mother what that advertisement meant. She laughed too. So it joined my list of strange things, to be hung with some others on the elder tree in Garvey's garden.

Another memorable advertisement was for bottom paper. I wondered why it showed a lovely, long car and not a bucking bronco, for it said: 'Even the wealthiest cannot buy better than Bronco toilet paper.' (And even the cleverest cannot answer all of Jeremy Paxman's questions.)

Many years later my mother told me that my fondness for reading was useful to her in times of sickness. It is sometimes hard for a mother to tell when a child is really ill or simply in need of a little extra attention. She said she had a sure way of telling with me. If I wasn't reading I was certainly sick. Once I started reading again I was better.

When I left home in 1943 my long word search came to an end. I found a library.

Notes

[41] Alban Butler: an English priest (1710–73). His *Lives of the Saints* was published in the years 1756–59. It has remained in print ever since.

[42] Androcles: a Roman slave who removed a thorn from a lion's paw. When Androcles was later thrown into the arena, the lion began to caress him. Both were set free. George Bernard Shaw used this story in his play, *Androcles and the Lion* (1912).

[43] Pre-Beijing/Mumbai days: in the days before English versions of foreign place names were tampered with for no good reason. The pun here is on the word 'Spree', which in Irish is a drinking binge, as well as being the name of a German river.

The Search for Enlightenment

I sometimes wonder if Peggy Hanley and I were unconsciously putting the Nurse Noonan theory to the test that day we went on the baby hunt. At some point I began to think about the way she did her job. Having found a baby, how did she decide which family to give it to? Then one day a red-haired woman with freckles came into the shop. She had her little girl with her. It was a red-haired little girl with freckles. So that was it. Nurse Noonan went by hair colour. If it was a bald baby some family had to take pot luck. Then there were the people who had none, like Patrick and Mrs Muldoon. They only had the dog, Conor. Perhaps they told her they didn't want any. But how could anyone not want a baby? I was still puzzled.

I don't know when or how I discovered the maternal angle but, as I've said already, I did know it by the time Margo was born in 1942. Then it fell to Margo herself to bring the subject out into the open a few years later. At the supper table one evening she silenced us all: 'I know where the kittens came from,' she said. 'The cat laid them.' We were stunned. Then my father surprised us even more, by saying softly, with a little wry smile, 'She did, Margo.' So that cat was out of the bag. But nothing more was said on the subject.

At first I assumed the baby began of its own accord. Partheno-genesis was what I had in mind – if I'd known that *paltóg*[44] then. I took another faltering step towards the final solution when Peggy Hanley started talking about some woman in the parish who'd had a baby. She spoke as if it were something blameworthy.

'But she can't help it,' I said.

'Of course she can help it,' retorted Peggy.

Still, that was all she said.

Then a chance remark I overheard made me wonder more and more. A customer said that someone was like his father. How could he be? I was getting an inkling that fathers just might have something to do with babies. I tried the dictionary and looked up 'male': the sex that begets young. That settled it. They did have something to do with them. Now I looked up 'beget': become the father of. That was the trouble with the dictionary sometimes – it took me on a Tony Lumpkin merry-go-round[45]. I got no further.

Finally, Catherine told me. She was far more explicit than the dictionary. I didn't believe her. Nice people like your father and mother wouldn't do a horrible thing like that. Neither would any of the other parents all around. Above all, you couldn't imagine Patrick and Mrs Muldoon, that saintly pair, doing such a castor-oily thing. They wouldn't! They couldn't! They didn't! Then suddenly my guts lurched. They had no children. So that was why. They didn't do this awful thing. Maybe Catherine was telling me the truth, after all. Could it possibly be?

Some days later, Kitty Hanrahan backed up Catherine's words, saying she thought it was a duty God gave them when they were married. So you could get out of it. If you didn't get married you were not given that dreadful duty. To be absolutely safe from it I'd become a nun.

The Hanleys had an Auntie Michael, a nun. They enjoyed a certain kudos from being the only children who had an auntie with a man's name. It occurred to me that perhaps all nuns had to have a man's name. In that case, I would be Sister John of the Cross. Then I remembered our own 'Auntie Nun', my mother's sister who lived in Texas.

'What is Auntie Nun's proper name?' I asked my mother.

'Sister Mary Anne,' said she.

You could have a woman's name then. I'd be Sister Mary of the Sacred Heart.

Anyway, now I knew. The search was over. Gradually, my revulsion faded. I saw that this Daddy–Mammy combination thing made sense and explained much. Awful as it seemed in itself, it was wonderful in its outcome. 'A terrible beauty' might have expressed my new view of it.[46]

I wonder now if my search would have been easier if we'd had an 'ethnic' element in Doonbeg.

Notes

[44] *paltóg*: Irish for a 'huge mouthful of a word'.

[45] Tony Lumpkin: a comic character in the play *She Stoops to Conquer* by Oliver Goldsmith (1728–74). Tony tricks his mother by driving her round in a circle, giving her the impression that she is moving forward.

[46] 'A terrible beauty': from the poem 'Easter 1916' by W B Yeats (1865–1939). He says that the men who died in the Rebellion

> Are changed, changed utterly;
> A terrible beauty is born.

Lysheen Again

One day during the Christmas holidays in 1943, Aunt Molly came again for me and I went to Lysheen with her. Obviously there had been some correspondence on the matter between her and my mother, although I'd heard nothing of it.

This time I was old enough to see how different my new surroundings were from those I was used to. I was also able to see how different Lysheen itself was from my early memories of it. After all, five years had passed.

The first change I noticed was in the house. The bedridden old woman was no longer there. Her room was now mine. Memories lingered but the odours had left. I was prepared to settle in. It was nice to have a room of my own. Somehow, though, my aunt and I got off to a slightly awkward start on my first night back.

'You go between the sheets,' she said, helping me into bed.

'I know,' I said, bridling. She was instantly apologetic.

'I just thought,' she explained, 'that your Mammy mightn't always have a clean top sheet ready.'

She happened to be right, as I remembered the occasional scratch of a rough blanket next to me. But I said nothing and the awkward moment passed.

If my uncle's mother had departed, the distant relative was still around. I was right to feel a little uneasy about her; I was about to get my comeuppance for my Actaeon[47] act of yesteryear.

One day I was playing in a field with some of the twelve Taaffe children, near neighbours of ours. There was a donkey in the field too. The Taaffes caught the animal and suggested I went for a ride on it. Although reluctant at first, I let them persuade me and help me up. Soon I was sitting comfortably and holding on. The next thing I knew, my spine was vibrating along its length and I was sitting on the grass, not comfortably at all. Two things must have happened together, unknown to me. The donkey had shot forward and I had shot down. The Taaffes were on the ground also, rolling around laughing. I struggled to my feet and dragged myself home.

Large, livid patches soon appeared where I fell and I was stiff and sore. Now whom did my aunt send for? Doctor? Nurse? Chemist? The answer is: none of these. She sent for Kitty-with-the-cure. So I was made to lie in bed on my front, bare bottom up, to receive Kitty's ministrations which took the form, I thought, of incantations and spells delivered in sepulchral tones at high speed. I couldn't make out a word. She also gave me a sprinkling of what I took then to be authentic Holy Water, but it was more likely to have been some brew of her own concoction. I was surprised that my aunt, a sane and sensible woman, seemed to believe in this hocus-pocus. Still, I have to admit that a faint taint of such belief came to me too. It seemed so remarkable that Kitty should have got her own back after all this time. I couldn't but wonder if she really had some secret power. Maybe the donkey was hers. Whether her treatment had any effect on my condition or not, who knows. It certainly achieved poetic justice for her.

Shortly after this, undeterred, I decided to try a different ride. I took my aunt's bike out one day and, after a few tumbles and wobbles, I became a cyclist.

The jobs for my aunt were very different from those I did at home. Pounding blankets became pounding the churn; a much more strenuous task. Then there was washing the separator – the piece of dairy equipment that separated the cream from the rest of the milk. It had innumerable parts which had to be meticulously washed and scoured and checked ad infinitum, then finally dried. It was the most tiresome work imaginable. And it had to be done every day.

The fruit garden was a mixed blessing. Besides apples, gooseberries and redcurrants, it produced blackcurrants, blackcurrants and blackcurrants. My aunt made huge amounts of blackcurrant jam, work which involved me in lengthy bouts of topping and tailing. I enjoyed picking the fruit, because as earlier with the wild blackberries around Doonbeg, I ate as I picked. But I felt like screaming over the two 't's. The business seemed interminable.

My uncle's socks had to be darned, pile on pile of them. Then I wished Miss Hanrahan hadn't taught me how to darn. When I complained, as I did time and time again, my aunt would say that my cousin, another niece of hers who also stayed with her for a while, always did all her jobs with a much better grace. Clearly, she was a nicer niece. Incidentally, this cousin of mine became a nun. What better way to get out of sock-darning for life? This reminded me of my own thoughts about 'entering'.

When I returned home I asked my mother why there was no sock-darning in our house. She told me she had tried it once, '...but the darns hurt your father's feet... he found them too lumpy.' What a blessing, I thought.

Another job I was expected to do in Lysheen was to search the hedges and ditches for *fodhrán* to feed the pigs on. This was a hairy, rough-leaved plant that reddened my bare arms. I usually dawdled over this job, especially on a warm day.

I was conscious of enhanced social standing in Lysheen. In Doonbeg I was just one of the Tomelteys. Here I was Mrs Tierney's niece. There was a political element in this. The reflected glory came from my uncle who had taken an active part in the War of Independence and had been on hunger strike in prison. He drew a small State Pension as a reward. Unlike Márquez's Colonel[48], he had someone to write to him.

Notes

[47] Actaeon: In Greek mythology, Actaeon was a hunter who one day happened to see the goddess Artemis bathing in a stream. So that he could not afterwards boast that she had shown herself naked in his presence, she changed him into a stag. Then his own pack of hounds tore him to pieces.

[48] Márquez: The reference is to the story 'El Coronel no Tiene Quien Le Escriba' (1958) by the Colombian novelist Gabriel García Márquez, who received the Nobel Prize for Literature in 1982. This story is translated into English under the title 'No One Writes to the Colonel'. Fifty years after the war he served in, the Colonel is still waiting for the letter entitling him to his pension.

Inverkeel

I have no recollection of going to the nearby town on my first visit to Lysheen. This time the town loomed large in my life, for I went to school there. It was called Inverkeel. It was – and is – a holiday resort and very different from Doonbeg.

If in my home town almost every house was a public house, here almost every house was a guesthouse, for part of the year at least. There was a lovely, long beach, with pale sand as fine as salt. There were many sand hills. It was said that Funny Things happened in them. So the children of this town snooped, not on drunken men but on courting couples. They were more sophisticated than we!

Unlike Doonbeg, Inverkeel had a public library. My scraping and scratching for reading material was at an end. I went from Just William to William Le Queux. I hadn't yet met William S in person, only at second-hand, through the Lambs. During my Baroness Orczy period I had my second brush with the war.

As my father was still working in England, we wrote to each other fairly often. I usually included something about my current reading in my letters. I got a surprising answer to one such letter. My father told me he'd got my letter – or rather my half letter, as he put it. The censor had cut out the other half. It dawned on me that it must have been the bit I'd written about the Scarlet Pimpernel. I was quite amused to think I might have been suspected of spying or something. But I decided to avoid any reference to any kind of conflict in future letters. I would censor myself.

On sunny days I loved to read by the sea. Among the rocks I always found a sheltered little shelf that the wind couldn't reach. The shore was only a few minutes' walk from my aunt's.

Another big difference between the two towns lay in the public entertainment available. In Doonbeg we had occasional concerts and plays put on by the local talent and rare visits from travelling drama companies. In Inverkeel there were various performances most evenings throughout the holiday season. My aunt was fond of these shows and took me with her. Looking back, I think it was mostly slapstick and melodrama that was given. But we both enjoyed it.

School was very different from the one I'd left. The Principal was a nun, called Mother St Andrew. Her style was easy-going, friendly, and conversational. There was no slapping. Like Miss McGinty she loved singing. To start a session, she hit the edge of the table with her tuning fork. Then she sang, 'lah, ti, doh, soh, mi, doh.' That, apparently, took you into the key of E flat major. It was nice to know where I was, especially in an alien land. I was reminded on one occasion of a book title I'd seen in the library – *Murder in Flat Fourteen*. Hitherto, 'flat' to me was a matter of pancakes, bicycles tyres, and 'that's flat'. Still, if a musical note can be flat why not a number?

Little competitions, with little prizes, were a frequent occurrence in Mother St Andrew's regime. And she was keen on history, especially the French Revolution. As we were reading a book about Lord Edward Fitzgerald and his part in the 1798 Rebellion, some background knowledge of earlier events in France was essential. She made it fascinating. When I discovered the Scarlet Pimpernel books in the library I became keen too.

The Convent that Mother St Andrew belonged to had a day Secondary school, and it was understood in the family that I'd attend it on leaving the Primary school. But I rejected that plan. Among all the changes around me, I found I was changing myself. I was getting discontented, lazy and sullen. I wanted to go home.

'I won't stand in your way,' said my aunt.

She might well have said, 'I can't stand you any longer, anyway.' It was the beginning of the summer holidays, 1945. My father came home on holiday and set my aunt a telegram, the first I'd ever seen.

'MEETING MOLLY GALWAY MONDAY TIMMY,' it said. I was delighted when my aunt showed it to me. So she put me on the bus – there was only one service a day between Sligo and Galway – and my father duly met me. Although he'd never displayed affection openly and didn't now, I knew by his voice

and manner how happy he was to see me, as I was to see him. We
had lunch in a restaurant before catching the bus to Doonbeg.
That was another first for me, my first meal out.

My father's holiday soon ended and he went back to England.

The Convent of Mercy

Dara Hanley was, I think, the first of the Middle Street children to go to a Convent Boarding School. The rest of us were deeply impressed when she came home for the Christmas holidays able to say the Hail Mary in French. Then she told us a strange story about something they were reading with a person called Bottom[49] in it. How could the nuns allow that? It gave one pause. Maybe I should rethink a few things. But, of course, I wouldn't be going to the Convent. At the time, boarding school seemed out of the question for me. This was before my second visit to Aunt Molly's.

On my return my mother had to decide what to do with me. I was twelve and would have to go to school for a further two years. For me to go back to Doonbeg Primary was unthinkable. There was no Secondary School in the town at that time. In those days Secondary Education was only available to those who lived in large towns with day Secondary Schools, or to those whose parents could afford to send them to boarding schools. I belonged to neither category. My mother decided to send me to Dagoolan Mercy Convent School as a day pupil. Dagoolan is about nine miles from Doonbeg. The idea of my cycling there was considered but rejected. I would go by bus. However, the only service available got me to school halfway through the second lesson, and after school I had to hang around town for quite a while, waiting for the bus home. I did that for a little more than two weeks. Then the miracle happened.

Sister Josephine, the Head of the school, got in touch with my mother and invited her to come and see her to discuss the possibility of my boarding at the school, as most girls did, except those who lived in the town of Dagoolan. My mother and Sister Josephine had their talk; the upshot of it was that I was taken on as a boarder, at ludicrously reduced fees. I'm afraid I didn't then appreciate fully the extraordinary generosity of Sister Josephine to my mother and me. I became a boarder the following week.

My mother found it hard to provide me with the uniform and to equip me with all the blankets, linen and things on the list Sister had given her. But she did. I was ecstatic. For the first time in my life I owned a dressing gown. It was of grey flannel, with purple piping. I had an under-blanket. We never had that at home. I had a white damask coverlet which I loved. I still have it, more that sixty years later. I come across it in the attic from time to time. My name is still quite clear in one corner in marking ink.

I had now entered a strange new world: a world of serviettes, serviette rings, soup spoons, three-course meals, delicious little supper dishes, hot water on tap, central heating and more and more and more. All in all, to me it was gracious living.

I took at once to the orderly routine of a fully planned day. Some girls found periods of silence irksome. I didn't. I loved the tranquil atmosphere. And I was at peace again. The agitation I'd felt latterly at Aunt Molly's left me completely. The spiky adolescent lurking in the offing like a shark's fin dropped out of sight, and the shyness of my early childhood came back. I suppose I felt overwhelmed. This shyness must have come across as insincerity, for one nun called me a little bundle of affectation, in a moment of exasperation at my supposed shy act.

Sister Josephine was the life and soul of the school; a powerful presence there. She may have had a sharp tongue and an intimidating manner, but she had a warm heart, as well I knew. Although we were all a little afraid of her, I'm convinced the whole school had a sneaking regard for her. This was demonstrated in dramatic fashion during a performance of an operetta, put on by the music nuns. A reference to the Empress Josephine brought on a thunderous burst of prolonged applause, everyone's eyes fixed on Sister. She appeared to enjoy the adulation, if embarrassed by it. I think she was a source of wry amusement to the other nuns.

From time to time she lectured us on the condition of our uniforms. She fussed particularly about hats, gloves and shoes. What fun, thought I, if, one Sunday, we all turned out for our walk in well-brushed hats, elegant gloves, shining shoes – and nothing else. She liked to compare our neglect of our school clothes with our smart appearance during holidays, when we were apt to call in, dressed up, as she phrased it, 'like Lady Ardagh and Clonmacnoise.'

I must, on one occasion, have given her some specious answer to something; some apparently plausible explanation. She looked hard at me.

'You're very glib,' she said. 'You should become a lawyer. When you don't know the right answer you come up with something that sounds like a better one.'

A funny thing happened that first term, soon after my arrival. We had a holiday, to celebrate the feast of Our Lady of Mercy. Everyone was free to wander round the buildings or grounds. Angela Kiely and I repaired to a music room, one of a suite on a quiet corridor. Suddenly, the door flew open and a flushed and flustered Sister Immaculata burst in.

'Have you seen the Perpetual Marriage?' she asked.

'No, S'ter,' we answered in unison and consternation.

She flounced out. Angela and I looked at each other. What had we missed?

'What Perpetual Marriage?' said I. 'Every marriage is perpetual, isn't it?' (We all knew the basics by then.)

'Maybe it's some kind of tableau or procession or profession of novices,' suggested Angela.

'Maybe,' I ventured, 'it's something to do with that picture "The Mystic Marriage of St Catherine of Siena".'

'They could be doing a tableau of that,' said Angela.

Whatever it was, we hoped to catch at least the tail end of it. We hurried out.

Scurrying along the corridor towards us came Sister Immaculata hauling a reluctant Perpetua O'Mara to her piano lesson. Angela and I looked at each other again. Grin and chagrin! Great minds...

Because of an uncanny connection with the foregoing, I'll allow myself to flash-forward to a somewhat similar piece of confusion. Shortly after I started trying to teach, I met another young woman on a train. We started talking and soon found out we were in the same profession.

'Do you use Keys in Air in your school?' she asked me.

'No, we don't,' I replied. Nor quails in aspic, I thought.

Some time later, on learning of a Belgian inspector of schools called Cuisenaire, I remembered the stranger on the train[50]. And the connection? Her name was Felicity, joining up nicely with Perpetua. Those old fogies familiar with the Tridentine Mass will know that Perpetua and Felicity were always mentioned together in the Canon. They were young women, martyred in the reign of Septimius Severus[51].

When I went home for the Christmas holidays after my first term our house looked incredibly small. I stayed at Dagoolan Convent for two years. Then I moved to another Mercy Convent, an associated Community, in the next county. I was even happier there. In fact, I look on the four years I spent there as some of the happiest of my life.

Notes

[49] Bottom: a weaver, is a comic character in Shakespeare's *A Midsummer Night's Dream*.

[50] Stranger on a train: This is the title of the first novel of Patricia Highsmith (1921–95). Published in 1950, it was later made into a very successful film, directed by Alfred Hitchcock.

[51] Perpetua and Felicity: Vivia Perpetua was a young married woman of good social position. Felicity, also married, was a slave. Imprisoned for their faith with other Christians and catechumens at Carthage, they were thrown to the wild beasts in the amphitheatre on 7 March, AD 203. Their story is told by the theologian Tertullian and by an eyewitness.

A Brush with the Law

It was during my first term at the Convent that my mother had her little brush with the law, although she didn't tell me about it until long afterwards. It was nothing to write to the Convent about, the nuns being as good at censorship as any War Office.

In Doonbeg, as, no doubt, in other places, it was a truth tacitly acknowledged that a man who'd spent the week toiling in the field must be in want of a Guinness on a Sunday morning. So, every Sunday after second Mass, a soft knock would cause a pub door to open quietly, wide enough to allow a furtive figure to sidle in, to join many shadowy shapes already in place. To put it plainly, every pub in the town did what you would call a roaring trade, if it hadn't been done so soundlessly. Speakeasy, indeed. At those times our shop was almost black-dark, as the wooden shutters on the two windows facing the street didn't let a chink of light in from that side. The only light came through the small yard window. So the atmosphere of 'secrecy' was enhanced by the gloom.

If the law did not acknowledge this truth, it often turned a blind eye. Unfortunately for my mother, it didn't always turn a blind eye. From time to time the guards would raid a pub or two, whenever they felt tired of moving the tinkers on, or catching cyclists without lights, or dog owners without licences, or berating a child who'd missed a day at school. So it came about that my mother was prosecuted for selling alcoholic drink after hours. She had to appear in court. The case was dismissed, much having been made of the six children and the absent father.

When relating the incident to me some time later, my mother sounded quite happy about it, less because of her acquittal than for the fact that the judge had referred to her as 'the young lady'. She would have been in her late thirties then. 'I must have looked very young,' she said. The judge's polite comment seemed to have compensated her for the ordeal.

At the time, cases like my mother's were cropping up all over the country. One of them may well have been the last straw that broke the back of that ass of a law, because not too long after that things changed and pubs were allowed to open on Sunday mornings.

A Real Childhood

'When I was a child I spoke as a child. I understood as a child. I thought as a child.'[52] I like to think that these words of Saint Paul applied to me and to the children I grew up with. Do they apply to many children today?

It seems to me that some children nowadays are not given enough time to be children. They are allowed little real leisure. Even their play is organised, structured, supervised. They 'have no time to stand and stare.'[53] We had plenty. Although we were kept under strict control at home and at school, when playing out of doors we were completely free. If there was any organising, we did it ourselves. Even at school there was no teacher on duty in the schoolyard. An occasional tap on a window, however, showed they were keeping an eye, so that anything ugly was nipped in the bud.

Too much reliance on gadgets and equipment gives children little opportunity to make their own amusements. Incentives are wanting. Lacking 'aids', we were left to our own devices and had to exert ourselves more. There was nothing passive about our play. And I'm convinced we were less apt to complain of boredom. When put to it, a child can make a game of any activity, a toy out of any object. The best thing to tell a child is to go out and play – and go empty-handed. After all, isn't that what children do? Play.

We had freedom to roam the town and its environs. Of course, there was next to no traffic so that parents had few worries on that score. There was no need to tell us not to speak to strangers. There weren't any. We even knew the tinkers who came and went. We lived in a close, settled community in which everyone knew everyone else. We had social cohesion with a vengeance. But this is no longer the case in Doonbeg. Housing estate anonymity has descended on it.

In the matter of dress, children, especially girls, are often not allowed to look like children. There doesn't seem to be the clear distinction there used to be between adults' clothes and children's. Many shops display only adult styles cut down to size. One sees, with dismay, little girls going about in skimpy scraps of lurid colour and decked out in garish glitter. Surely, children's clothes should be quiet, simple and ample.

Something else that, to my mind, does nothing to enhance the quality of childhood today is what I see as the undue prominence given to early 'sex education'. I see no need whatever for such a subject in primary schools, certainly not before the age of ten. Of course, if children ask they should be told – at home. But why thrust 'adult' information on them? Admittedly, parents in the past went to risible lengths to keep children from this knowledge. Now, however, I believe things have gone to the other extreme. There's anecdotal evidence that children may be unable to take such knowledge in. I heard of a little girl who, when told that a lady had a baby in her tummy, simply laughed at the idea. 'Oh no,' she said, 'it's a box of chocolates.' Clearly, 'pull the other one' was her response.

Anyway, I wouldn't be without the memory of that Baby Quest for all the 'sex education' in the world.

Here endeth the sermon of the Grumpy Old Woman.

Notes

[52] Saint Paul: The quotation is from the New Testament, the First Epistle of Saint Paul to the Corinthians, Chapter 13, verse 11.

[53] No time to stand and stare: This quotation is from the poem 'Leisure' by W H Davies (1871–1940), *Classic Favourite Poems*, edited by Charles Osborne, Harper Perennial, 2005 (reprinted by permission of the Executors of the W H Davies Estate and Jonathan Cape Ltd). A short poem (fourteen lines), it is much anthologised. It begins:

> What is this life if, full of care,
> We have no time to stand and stare.

Memory

> The light of other days
> Keeps flashing on my mind;
> I'll be in thrall to these bright rays,
> Till Someone draws the blind!

Nowadays I recall things long past much more readily than recent things. It must be that when we are new to the world and everything is a 'first', the impressions made on the mind are deep, indelible and always within reach. Our grip on reality is so tenacious because it is absolutely vital. Even so, we don't, of course, remember everything. I see memory as a starry sky, splashes of light against a dark background. Some splashes are big and bright, others small and dim. Some things I recall very clearly, others are faint and uncertain. I seem to remember best things I felt strongly about and also things that baffled me.

It's hardly surprising that I remember distinctly our father's goodbye to Catherine and me the evening before he left home to work in England. We didn't see him leave the house the next morning. He must have gone before we got up. Such a momentous event in family life is naturally unforgettable. Why, though, does the memory retain so many trivial things? Or what makes it retain some, while letting the rest go? Like William Allingham's 'Four Ducks on a Pond'[54], many little things are unaccountably kept in mind.

In *Mansfield Park*, Jane Austen has Fanny Price eulogising the faculty of memory in a way I find wholly convincing. Here is a little of her eulogy:

> If any one faculty of our nature may be called more wonderful
> that the rest, I do think it is memory... We are to be sure a
> miracle in every way – but our powers of recollecting and
> forgetting do seem peculiarly past finding out.

At present I do more forgetting than recollecting where recent events are concerned. The name of an acquaintance I meet on the street often eludes me until the person has passed by. There's a time lag between recognition and recollection. It's like lightning first, then thunder! If I'm ironing a shirtsleeve and pause to ask myself if this is the first sleeve or the second, I rarely know. I always hope it's the second!

I feel glad my childhood memories are pleasant, on the whole. Even the less pleasant things have long since lost their power to hurt. So I revel in them all. Indeed, I live in them. I look back in gratitude, with a full heart, saying in the words of the Psalmist:

I thank You for the wonder of my being.[55]

Notes

[54] 'Four Ducks on a Pond': a poem by William Allingham (1824–89). Just six lines:

> Four ducks on a pond,
> A grass-bank beyond,
> A blue sky of spring
> What a little thing
> To remember for years –
> To remember with tears!

[55] 'I thank You for the wonder of my being': quotation from the Bible, Old Testament, Book of Psalms, Psalm 138.